A Treasury of Saints

DAVID SELF

LION

Published by Lion Books
an imprint of
Lion Hudson plc
Wilkinson House, Jordan Hill Road,
Oxford OX2 8DR, England
www.lionhudson.com/lion

ISBN 978 0 7459 6457 7

First edition 2014

Acknowledgments
The author acknowledges the assistance he has received from the Saint George Orthodox Information Service.

Scripture quotations are taken or adapted from the Good News Bible © 1994 published by the Bible Societies/HarperCollins Publishers Ltd UK, Good News Bible © American Bible Society 1966, 1971, 1976, 1992. Used with permission.

A catalogue record for this book is available from the British Library

Printed and bound in China, December 2013, LH06

Contents

MARY 5

JOSEPH, JOACHIM, ANNE, ZECHARIAH, AND
 ELIZABETH 9

JOHN THE BAPTIST 13

JESUS' DISCIPLES 18

ANDREW 23

MATTHEW 27

JOHN 31

SIMON PETER 35

THE MARYS 43

THOMAS 47

STEPHEN 51

PAUL 55

BARNABAS, TIMOTHY, AND TITUS 63

JOHN MARK AND LUKE 67

CLEMENT AND IGNATIUS OF ANTIOCH 71

LAWRENCE, VALENTINE, AND SEBASTIAN 75

GEORGE 83

CHRISTOPHER 87

CATHERINE OF ALEXANDRIA 91

CONSTANTINE AND HELENA 95

NICHOLAS 99

BASIL THE GREAT AND GREGORY NAZIANZEN 103

MARTIN OF TOURS 107

AUGUSTINE OF HIPPO 111

PATRICK   115

BRIGID   119

BENEDICT   123

DAVID   127

COLUMBA OF IONA AND KENTIGERN   131

GREGORY, AUGUSTINE OF CANTERBURY, AND
  ETHELBERT   137

AIDAN, OSWALD, AND HILDA OF WHITBY   141

CUTHBERT   147

BEDE   151

BONIFACE   155

MARGARET OF SCOTLAND   159

BERNARD OF CLAIRVAUX   163

THOMAS BECKET   167

FRANCIS OF ASSISI   171

CLARE AND ANTONY OF PADUA   177

THOMAS AQUINAS   181

CATHERINE OF SIENA   185

THOMAS MORE   189

IGNATIUS OF LOYOLA   193

FRANCIS XAVIER   197

ELIZABETH ANN SETON   201

JOHN BOSCO   205

BERNADETTE SOUBIROUS   209

THÉRÈSE OF LISIEUX   213

GABRIEL AND MICHAEL   217

CALENDAR OF SAINTS' DAYS   221

Mary

SAINT'S DAYS

Mary is remembered on several
days of the year:

2 FEBRUARY
The Presentation of the Lord
(or Mary's Thanksgiving)

25 MARCH
The Annunciation

15 AUGUST
The Assumption

8 SEPTEMBER
Her birthday

8 DECEMBER
The Immaculate Conception

As the mother of Jesus, Mary has always been considered important among the saints. Some information about her life can be found in the Bible. For example, we know she was alive when Jesus was crucified. Other ancient sources indicate that she was a teenager when she gave birth to Jesus. Some Christians (mainly Catholic and Orthodox) ask Mary to pray to God for them, and many respectfully refer to her as "Our Lady". Mary's special days of the year include the Annunciation (the announcing by Gabriel of the birth of Jesus), the Assumption (her entry into heaven after her death), and the Immaculate Conception (remembering the belief of some Christians that Mary was born without sin).

SHE WAS A teenager. Engaged to be married to Joseph – a decent, hard-working guy. Now, as she worked in her mother's kitchen, she started daydreaming about their married life together. They would have their own house, there in Nazareth. He'd carry on his business as a carpenter. Things looked good. But then the angel turned up.

"Peace be with you," he said. "Don't be afraid."

Easier said than done.

"The Lord God has blessed you," continued the angel, whose name was Gabriel. "You're going to become pregnant. You'll give birth to a son and you'll name him Jesus. People will say he is the Son of God. He'll be like a king and he'll reign for ever and ever."

Mary felt weak. "How can this be? Joseph and I aren't... we aren't married yet. I'm still a virgin."

"God's Holy Spirit will come upon you. God will be the father of your child. There's nothing God can't do."

And that is what happened. Mary became pregnant; Joseph stood by her; they got married.

And when her time came, Mary gave birth to a boy. But not at home in Nazareth. It happened in Bethlehem, a faraway town. But, yes, they did name him Jesus, and later, she went to the Temple to make a thanksgiving for the birth of God's Son.

Like his foster father, Joseph, Jesus probably became a carpenter. He worked in Nazareth until he was about thirty. For the next three years, he was to travel around the country, teaching, healing people who were ill, and doing all kinds of wonderful things.

And whatever he did, Mary was always there for him. When friends were married in a town named Cana, not far from Galilee, both Mary and Jesus were guests. Later, Mary went to Jerusalem with him for what was to be the week before his crucifixion. That week, she suffered the pain of seeing her own son after he had been beaten and tormented by the Roman soldiers. She had to watch him drag his heavy cross through the streets of Jerusalem, and she saw him hang on the cross until he died.

But when things seemed to be going so terribly, painfully wrong, she always had that secret in her heart, the message brought to her by the angel Gabriel – she had been chosen by God to be the mother of his Son. In those difficult times, she could remember the words she'd said just after Gabriel had first brought her the news...

My heart praises the Lord; my soul is glad because of God my Saviour, for he has remembered me, his lowly servant! From now on all people will call me happy, because of the great things the Mighty God has done for me. His name is holy; from one generation to another he shows mercy to those who honour him.

He has stretched out his mighty arm and scattered the proud with all their plans. He has brought down mighty kings from their thrones, and lifted up the lowly. He has filled the hungry with good things, and sent the rich away with empty hands.

LUKE 1:46–53

Joseph, Joachim, Anne, Zechariah, and Elizabeth

The Holy Family

SAINTS' DAYS

19 MARCH
Joseph

1 MAY
Joseph the Worker

26 JULY
Joachim and Anne

5 NOVEMBER
Zechariah and Elizabeth

9

When people talk of the "holy family", they usually mean Joseph, Mary, and Jesus. We know a lot about Mary, but what about Joseph and other relatives? According to tradition, Joseph was an old man when he married Mary. The stories of Mary's parents, Joachim and Anne, are found in the Gospel of James (written in the second century and not part of the Bible). We only know about Zechariah and Elizabeth from Luke's Gospel. In 1933, the pope made 1 May the festival of "Joseph the Worker", a day on which many people remember all workers.

JOSEPH

IT MUST HAVE been so confusing for Joseph. He was just about to wed Mary when he discovered she was pregnant. He knew he wasn't the father of her baby and decided to leave her quietly so that people wouldn't gossip. Before he could do this, an angel appeared to him.

"Joseph," said the angel, "don't be afraid to marry Mary. The son she is going to have has been given to her by the Holy Spirit of God. You will name him Jesus, and he will save people from their sins."

It was a lot to take in for Joseph, an ordinary carpenter living in the town of Nazareth. But he did wed Mary.

When the Romans held a census to work out who had to pay taxes, Joseph took Mary to Bethlehem, which used to be his hometown. It was while they were there that Jesus was born. When Joseph realized the baby was in danger from King Herod, he took the family to safety in Egypt. Some time later, they returned to Nazareth.

Joseph was still looking after his family when Jesus was twelve years old and the family went to Jerusalem. After that, no more is heard of him.

When Jesus was being crucified, he told John, one of his disciples, to look after his mother, Mary. Many say that this shows that Joseph must have died.

JOACHIM AND ANNE

THE BIBLE SAYS that the name of Joseph's father was either Jacob or Heli, but there is no mention of Mary's parents. However, there are various stories about them and they are usually given the names of Joachim and Anne.

It is said that when they were quite old, Joachim went into the desert to pray that they might have a child. Anne went to the Temple and prayed for the same blessing. An angel appeared and said to her, "Anne, the Lord God has heard your prayers and you shall indeed become pregnant and have a baby.

You must name her Mary, and she will be spoken about all over the world." An angel also appeared to Joachim. Nine months later, the baby was born.

ZECHARIAH AND ELIZABETH

ELIZABETH WAS A much older relative of Mary – too old to have children. But six months before Mary became pregnant with Jesus, Elizabeth also became pregnant. Her husband, Zechariah, who was a priest, saw an angel who said the child should be named John. At that moment, Zechariah lost the power of speech. When Elizabeth gave birth, everyone said the boy should be named Zechariah, like his father. But Elizabeth said he should be named John – and Zechariah wrote down the words "His name is John". Then Zechariah was able to speak again. The boy grew up to be known as John the Baptist.

Our God is merciful and tender.
He will cause the bright dawn of salvation
to rise on us
and to shine from heaven on all those who live
in the dark shadow of death,
to guide our steps into the path of peace.

FROM ZECHARIAH'S PROPHECY ON THE BIRTH OF JOHN,
LUKE 1:78–79

John the Baptist

SAINT'S DAYS

24 JUNE
His birthday

29 AUGUST
The beheading of John is remembered on this day.

John the Baptist was the son of Zechariah and his
wife, Elizabeth, who was the cousin of Mary, the
mother of Jesus. John was born six months before Jesus.
When he grew up, he preached by the River Jordan
and he baptized many people, including Jesus. He is
sometimes called "the forerunner of Jesus" – the one
who came before Jesus to prepare people to hear Jesus.
Most saints are remembered on the day they died, but
John is usually remembered on his birthday.

EVERYONE WANTED TO SEE John – a weird man
dressed in a simple tunic made out of camel's
hair and tied with a leather belt around his waist.
He lived in the desert, some way from Jerusalem
and near the River Jordan.

As far as people could tell, he lived on honey and
locusts, which are insects, a bit like grasshoppers,
that are carried by the warm desert winds.

People came from all around, curious to see this
man who looked as they imagined the prophets had
looked in olden times. They also thought he might
be the promised one, the messiah whom God had
said would one day come to save the people from
all their troubles.

They didn't come just to look. They also came to
listen.

"Give up your sinful ways. Be baptized and God

will forgive you for all the wrongs you've done."

Many people were baptized by John. Once they'd said they were sorry for their sins, he would lead them into the River Jordan and lower them into the water for a moment as a sign that they wished their sins were washed away. But they knew this was not enough.

"What else must we do?" the people asked the man they knew as John the Baptist.

"Whoever has two shirts must give one away to a man who hasn't got one – and whoever has enough food must share it."

Some tax collectors came to be baptized. "Teacher," they asked, "what must we do?"

"Don't collect more tax than you're supposed to," John replied.

That made the crowds smile because the tax collectors were famous for demanding more than they should.

Then some soldiers said, "What about us?"

"Don't make false accusations and don't take money from people by force. Be content with your pay."

All this made people wonder more and more if John was the messiah they were waiting for. When John realized what they were saying, he immediately denied it.

"I baptize you with water but someone is coming who is much greater than I am. I'm not good enough even to undo his sandals. He will baptize you with God's Holy Spirit."

And indeed, very soon after this, Jesus came to be baptized by John. The two men had known each other when they were young because they were cousins.

John now looked at Jesus and understood who he really was. He turned and spoke to the crowds. "This is the one I was talking about when I said someone was coming who'd be much greater than I am. I didn't know who it would be, but now I know." John then turned to Jesus. "I ought to be baptized by you," he said.

"No," said Jesus. "You must baptize me because in that way, we shall do what God wants."

So John baptized Jesus in the River Jordan. As John lifted Jesus up out of the water, it seemed as if a light settled on Jesus, almost like a white dove coming down from the sky. Both John and Jesus believed that it was the Holy Spirit and that God was pleased with what had been done.

Ever since, John has been known as the "forerunner" of Jesus, the one who prepared the way for Jesus to begin his work on earth.

After John had baptized Jesus, he continued to preach in the desert. He also started speaking out against the local ruler, Herod Antipas (the son of Herod who had tried to kill the baby Jesus).

Herod had divorced his wife and married Herodias, who was both his niece and the wife of his half-brother Philip. John said that Herod was wrong to marry her, so Herod had John put in prison. He didn't dare have him killed because John was so popular, but Herodias wanted John dead.

She got her chance on the day of Herod's birthday. Herodias had her daughter, Salome, perform a dance for Herod. The way she did this so pleased Herod that he rashly said she could have whatever she wanted.

Salome and her mother had a whispered conversation.

"What should I ask for?" said Salome.

"The head of John the Baptist," Herodias replied.

Herod was very upset when he heard this. Even so, he sent a soldier to the prison. John was beheaded, and the soldier placed John's head on a tray and brought it back to Salome, who gave it to her mother.

Jesus' Disciples

SAINTS' DAYS

27 DECEMBER
John

1 MAY
Philip and James in the Anglican Churches

3 MAY
Philip and James in the Roman Catholic Church

29 JUNE
Simon, later named Peter

3 JULY
Thomas

Saints' Days

25 JULY
James, son of Zebedee

24 AUGUST
Bartholomew (Nathaniel)

21 SEPTEMBER
Matthew

28 OCTOBER
Simon from Cana and Thaddeus (Jude)

30 NOVEMBER
Andrew

Eleven of Jesus' twelve special followers (disciples)
became known as saints. They were: Simon, later
known as Peter, and his brother Andrew; James and
John, whose father's name was Zebedee; Matthew;
Thomas; Philip; James, sometimes known as James
the Less; Bartholomew, also known as Nathaniel;
Simon from Cana, also known as Simon the Zealot;
Thaddeus, also known as Jude and said to be the
brother of James the Less. The twelfth disciple (who is
not a saint) was Judas Iscariot, who betrayed Jesus.

WE NEED A new boat," said Simon.
    "We can't afford a new boat," said
Andrew.

Simon and Andrew were brothers, and they were
both fishermen.

"What about James and John?" asked Simon.
"They need a new boat. If we joined up with them,
we could afford a boat between us."

The four fishermen agreed and asked the local
boat builder to build it for them.

As soon as it was finished, they wanted to try it
out. The best time of day for catching fish was at
night. So in the late evening, they pushed their new
boat onto Lake Galilee. They rowed a little way
out, took down the sail, and threw their fishing nets
into the sea. Early next morning, as it was getting

light, they pulled the ends of the nets together and sailed back to the shore.

And that's what they did every night. Of course, their work wasn't over when they brought their catch ashore. They had to sort and clean the fish and pack them in wooden barrels with salt to stop them going bad. Then the fish were sold and the money was divided among the four of them.

One day, when they were sorting out their nets, Jesus came to that place. He started teaching the people there about helping and loving each other and not arguing. More people came to listen and they all crowded around. He asked the four friends if he could get in their boat and if they'd row him a little way from the shore. Jesus then sat at one end of their boat and was able to talk to all the people without being jostled.

After he'd finished talking, he told the four fishermen to row out to the middle of the lake. "Now put out your nets," he said.

Simon wasn't eager. They'd been fishing all night and had caught very little. But Jesus convinced them, so they did what he said. They caught more fish than they'd ever caught before – even though it was daytime!

When they got back to the shore, Simon, Andrew, James, and John decided there really was something very special about this man Jesus. They made up their minds to give up being fishermen and go with him from place to place, while he talked to people about looking after each other and about God's love. They were the first people to follow Jesus – and were part of the group of twelve special disciples Jesus chose from all the many men and women who became his followers.

One of the important lessons Jesus taught them was that they should not try to be better than one another, but should find ways to serve one another. At the last meal he shared with them before his death on the cross, he showed what that might mean by doing the work of a servant and washing their feet.

But what happened to their fishing boat? All we know is that, in 1986, a boat just like theirs was dug out of the mud at the edge of Lake Galilee.

Andrew

Saint's Day

30 November

According to tradition, Saint Andrew was crucified on an X-shaped cross, known as a saltire cross. Saint Andrew is the patron saint of Scotland, so the flag of Scotland shows a white saltire, or Saint Andrew's cross, on a blue background. The blue is a reminder that Andrew spent much of his life near the sea. Andrew is also the patron saint of Greece and of Russia, but there is no proof that he ever visited Russia or Scotland in his lifetime.

E VERYTHING SEEMED ORDINARY. An ordinary house near Lake Galilee. An ordinary family with two grown-up sons who were part of the family fishing business. But in the end, nothing was ordinary for these brothers, Simon and Andrew.

John's Gospel tells us that Simon and Andrew were already followers of John the Baptist when they decided to leave everything and follow Jesus. This Gospel also says that Andrew met Jesus before Simon did. For this reason, Andrew is sometimes named "the first disciple".

Andrew is mentioned several times in the Gospel story. Along with his brother Simon and the brothers James and John, he seems to have been among the closest followers of Jesus.

One day, a huge crowd of people had followed Jesus out into a desert place to hear him speak.

After many hours, it became clear that the people were hungry and had nothing to eat. Andrew noticed that one boy in the crowd had a basket containing five loaves and two fish. He brought him to Jesus, who blessed the food and shared it out among the thousands of people. Amazingly, everyone had enough to eat.

When Andrew and the others left their jobs as fishermen to become his disciples, Jesus said he would make them "fishers of men". After the end of Jesus' life on earth, Andrew (like the other disciples) started to travel widely, telling people all about Jesus. In this way, Andrew became a "fisherman" for Jesus – "catching" people and bringing them good news.

One story suggests that Andrew visited a place named Patras in Achaia (an ancient name for the southern part of mainland Greece). There Andrew persuaded the wife of an important Roman official named Egeas to become a Christian. Her name was Maximilla. The servant of her brother Stratocles also became a Christian.

This didn't please Egeas. He had Andrew beaten and thrown into prison. Then Egeas said that Andrew should be put to death by being crucified on the seashore.

When it came time for the crucifixion, Andrew

wasn't nailed to the cross. He was simply tied to it very tightly by a rope.

He stayed alive for two days, preaching. More than two thousand people came to listen and many of them became Christians.

Eventually, Andrew became so weak he died. Maximilla and the servant of Stratocles came and took down his body, washed it lovingly, and buried it properly.

Many years later, in the fourth century, a man named Regulus had a dream in which he was told to carry the remains (or relics) of Saint Andrew "to the ends of the earth". Along with a small group of friends, so the story goes, he journeyed from Greece to Scotland – a dangerous voyage in those days. They landed on the east coast of Scotland, built a church near to where they landed, and buried the relics of Saint Andrew under the church. The seaside city that now stands in that place is known as St Andrews. Saint Regulus (also known as Saint Rule) is remembered on 17 October.

Matthew

Saint's Day

21 SEPTEMBER

Matthew is famous because one of the Gospels in the Bible (which describe the life of Jesus) bears his name. However, it is unlikely that he wrote it: most people believe it wasn't written before the year 70 and perhaps not even until the year 105. Also, whoever wrote Matthew's Gospel borrowed quite a bit from Mark's Gospel. Matthew the taxman wouldn't have needed to do this because he would have known first-hand all that Jesus said and did.

J UST SUPPOSE... for years, your family has lived in the same land. Then, without warning, a foreign army arrives. The soldiers are everywhere, issuing orders, seizing food and property, taking control. They demand money – taxes. Taxes that have to be paid regularly to provide money for their army, for the foreign governor who's been sent to rule your country, and for a faraway emperor you've never seen.

So what would you think of the man who collects these taxes? Obviously he wouldn't be very popular. But suppose he was a local man? Think how despised he'd be!

That's how it was in Galilee in the time of Jesus. The Romans had invaded the country and they used local Galileans to collect their taxes. They had a little booth in the marketplace to which you had to take your regular payment. And you only had the taxman's word about how much you owed. Many people were sure that these tax collectors were charging more than they should and were keeping the extra for themselves. So unpopular were these taxmen that the local people thought they and their houses were "dirty". You never went near them if you could avoid it and you certainly didn't visit them at home.

There was one such collector in the town of Capernaum on the north-west coast of Lake Galilee, not far from where Andrew, Simon, James, and John had been fishermen. His name was Levi.

He'd heard about this new preacher and healer, Jesus. So he was curious when Jesus came past with his usual crowd of followers. But when Jesus came close to Levi's tax booth, all he said was, "Follow me."

Amazingly, that's what Levi did. He just got up, left his valuable job and income, and followed Jesus. Plenty of the crowd thought this was extraordinary, not because Levi had given up the chance of wealth, but because Jesus wanted such a person to be among his followers. But Jesus said, "I didn't come just to save good people. I came to help everyone."

Later, there was a supper at a tax collector's

house. It may have been Levi's house. Several taxmen were there, and so were Jesus and his close friends. This caused a lot of gossip.

"What sort of person would want to be seen with such terrible people?"

"Why does Jesus want to eat in the house of a man who's betrayed his own country by working for the Romans?"

Jesus told them, "Those who are healthy don't need a doctor." By this, he meant he had come to save wrongdoers, the ones most in need of his help.

Jesus gave Levi a new name to mark the start of his new life. He named him Matthew, which means "gift from God". Matthew became one of his twelve closest followers. He stayed with Jesus throughout the time that Jesus spent journeying around the country and was with him on his last journey to Jerusalem.

It's unclear what happened to Matthew after the Gospels say that Jesus returned to heaven. Many people believe that he journeyed far away, possibly to Ethiopia or Persia (modern-day Iran), in order to baptize people and to teach everyone he met that Jesus was with them always, until the end of time.

John

SAINT'S DAY

27 DECEMBER

John is often mentioned in the Bible. However, "John" could be as many as three separate people: 1 John the disciple, whom Jesus loved; 2 John the Evangelist, who wrote John's Gospel and possibly all or most of the Epistles (letters) of John, which are part of the New Testament; 3 John the Divine, who wrote the last book of the Bible, Revelation (a vision of heaven) and was kept prisoner on the Mediterranean island of Patmos.

I WANT YOU to get everything ready for the Passover meal," said Jesus to Peter and John.

"Where do you want us to get it ready?" they asked.

It was a good question. For three years, Jesus and his disciples had been going around Galilee. Now they had come to Jerusalem for the Passover festival when Jews have a special meal to remember their escape from slavery in Egypt. But although they were spending the week leading up to Passover in the city, they were staying with friends in a village named Bethany a few miles outside Jerusalem.

"As you go into the city, you'll meet a man carrying a water jar. Follow him to the house he goes into. He'll show you an upstairs room where you can get everything ready."

And that's exactly what happened. On the Thursday evening, Jesus and the twelve disciples met in that upstairs room for what was to be their last supper together. Nearest to Jesus was John.

John, along with his brother James, was among the first of the twelve disciples Jesus chose, and the two of them, together with Peter, seem to have been especially close to Jesus.

Once, a man named Jairus had come to Jesus to ask him to cure his daughter, who was seriously ill. By the time Jesus and his followers got to the house, they were told that the girl had died. Jesus reassured everyone that she was only sleeping. The crowd that had gathered didn't believe him. He chose just three disciples to go with him into the girl's room, where he woke her from the deep sleep she was in. Those three disciples were Peter, James – and John.

Another time, Jesus chose three disciples to go with him up a mountain, where he showed himself to them in all his heavenly glory. Again, the three chosen disciples were Peter, James – and John.

There seems to have been something special about John. He was almost certainly the youngest of the Twelve (he may have been only a teenager), and there is a possibility that he was a cousin of Jesus. This could explain why John is described as "the disciple Jesus loved" in the Gospel according to John.

John was incredibly loyal to Jesus. During the night following their last supper together, Jesus was arrested and put on trial. John alone appears to have been brave enough to find his way into the court room. And on the next day, when Jesus was hanging on the cross, the one disciple we know was there was John. It was John whom Jesus asked to care for his mother.

According to the Bible, after Jesus had returned to heaven, John and Peter worked together, spreading the message that Jesus had taught.

It is said that John lived to be a very old man and that he alone of the Twelve was not killed but died naturally. Many believe he spent his last years in a place named Ephesus, in what is now Turkey. When he got too old to preach, and people still came to hear him, he would simply say, "Love one another. That is the Lord's command. If you do that, it is enough."

Simon Peter

Saint's Day

29 June

Before Peter met Jesus, he was a fisherman named
Simon and lived in Bethsaida on the shore of Lake
Galilee. His father was named Jonas and he had a
brother, Andrew. Peter was one of the twelve disciples
and became especially close to Jesus. He probably
helped Mark write his Gospel and he may also have
helped write part of the first letter of Peter in the New
Testament. It is unlikely that the Aramaic-speaking
fisherman wrote it himself, since he probably would
not have been able to write Greek. It is almost certain
that Peter died in the year 64.

WHEN PEOPLE DIE, who lets them into heaven?
Many people would answer "Saint Peter"
because they picture him at the gates of heaven
with a bunch of keys, deciding who deserves to be
let in after their life on earth. It's easy to see why
people believe this.

One day, Jesus asked his disciples who people
thought he was.

"Some say you're John the Baptist," they
answered. "Others say you're one of the prophets
come back from olden times."

"But who do you think I am?" said Jesus.

"You're the Son of God," said Simon.

"Good for you, Simon," said Jesus. "I tell you,
you are indeed a rock, and on this rock, I will

build my church and I will give you the keys of the kingdom of heaven."

Jesus began to call him Peter, which means "rock". It was a kind of nickname, as if Jesus was calling him "Rocky" because he was such a solid, dependable kind of guy. Well, he was dependable in the end, but there was an important time when his courage seemed to fail.

It was in the Garden of Gethsemane, the night before Jesus was crucified. Jesus and his twelve disciples had had their last supper together in the upstairs room. The disciple named Judas Iscariot, who was going to betray Jesus, had disappeared, but Jesus and the other eleven had gone to Gethsemane to be quiet.

"Stay here," he said to eight of them. Then he led Peter and James and John a little way off. "Keep watch while I pray."

"Of course," said Peter. "You can rely on me."

Jesus went on a little further alone and lay down to pray. When he came back, he found they'd fallen asleep.

"Peter," he said sadly, "how is it that you couldn't keep watch even for one hour?"

This happened twice more. Each time Jesus went off to pray, Peter and the others failed to keep watch.

The third time, Jesus came back to them just as the traitor Judas brought the Temple guards to arrest Jesus. The disciples were completely outnumbered. Even so, Peter leaped to his feet, took out a sword he'd brought with him, and struck out at one of them – a slave named Malchus, who served the high priest. In fact, Peter sliced off his ear. Immediately, Jesus stopped the fighting and healed Malchus's wound, but within minutes, the guards had arrested Jesus and led him away.

Peter bravely followed, except he kept a safe distance behind. Earlier, he had promised he would never betray Jesus. Jesus hadn't believed his promise and had said that before cockcrow the next morning, he'd have denied knowing him three times.

Jesus was led into the house of the high priest to be put on trial. Peter followed, but stayed in the courtyard. Three times that night, people asked if he was one of Jesus' followers or if he knew him. Three times, Peter panicked and denied knowing him. The third time he did this, he heard the cock crow. Peter was heartbroken when he realized what he'd done.

Later that day, Jesus was crucified. John and several women followers of Jesus came to be near him as he suffered. No one knows where Peter was.

It was different the following Sunday, the first Easter Day. One of the women, Mary from Magdala, brought news to the disciples that the tomb in which Jesus' body had been buried was empty. Peter and John ran to the tomb. Not surprisingly, John (who was younger and fitter) got there first. He didn't dare go in, not knowing what he'd see. As soon as Peter arrived, he entered the tomb. He saw that the linen wrappings had been carefully folded. He went back to where the others were staying, amazed at what he'd seen. It wasn't long before he understood. It wasn't long before he lost all his doubts and cowardice. It wasn't long before he was the leader of all the disciples.

After Jesus' crucifixion and after he had risen from the dead, Jesus gave Peter a special instruction: "Feed my sheep." Jesus said this three times. He was telling Peter to be a guardian to all his followers, to look after them just as a shepherd looks after his sheep.

And indeed, after Jesus had gone back to heaven, Peter did become the leader of the disciples. One of the first things he did was to stand up in the middle of Jerusalem and preach to a huge crowd of people from many different countries. The man who had once been afraid to admit he was a follower of Jesus was now boldly standing up in the middle of the marketplace.

"Jesus, the one who was crucified, who was raised from the dead by the Lord God – he is the messenger, the redeemer God promised to send us. Now you must give up your wrongful ways, believe in him, and follow his teaching."

That day, after listening to Peter, about three thousand people became followers of Jesus.

In the years ahead, Peter did much to spread the word about Jesus. He healed people, he was sometimes put in prison, and he journeyed to many places in Palestine and Samaria, telling people wherever he went the good news about Jesus.

Later, there was some disagreement among Christians as to whether the message of Jesus was meant only for Jewish people or for all people. Peter argued very strongly that anyone could become a Christian – they didn't have be Jewish first.

It is widely believed that Peter journeyed to Rome and was put in prison there, along with several other Christians. This was in the time when the emperor of Rome was Nero, a cruel man who blamed Christians for anything that went wrong in his city.

A chance came for one of the prisoners to escape. The others tried to persuade Peter that it should be him. He hesitated but at last he agreed.

When he found himself outside prison, he set out to walk away from the city of Rome. Along the road, he met a shadowy figure carrying a cross. As he got nearer, he recognized the figure. It was Jesus.

"Where are you going?" asked Peter.

"I'm coming to be crucified a second time," said the figure.

Peter was so ashamed that he turned around, went back to Rome, and gave himself up. The order was given that he should be crucified, but he pleaded that he was unworthy to be crucified in the same way as Jesus. So, on 29 June in the year 64, Peter was crucified upside down in the arena where the Romans held circuses and other entertainments.

The great Church of Saint Peter in Rome is said to be built on the spot where his body was buried. Modern excavations suggest that the tomb of Saint Peter may indeed be in this place.

Peter is widely believed to be the author of two letters to new Christians, now in the Bible. Here are some of the instructions he gave them:

The end of all things is near. You must be self-controlled and alert, to be able to pray. Above everything, love one another earnestly, because love covers over many sins. Open your homes to each other without complaining. Each one, as a good manager of God's different gifts, must use for the good of others the special gift he has received from God. Whoever preaches must preach God's messages; whoever serves must serve with the strength that God gives, so that in all things praise may be given to God through Jesus Christ, to whom belong glory and power for ever and ever. Amen.

Do your best to add goodness to your faith; to your goodness add knowledge; to your knowledge add self-control; to your self-control add endurance; to your endurance add godliness; to your godliness add Christian affection; and to your Christian affection add love.

1 PETER 4:7–11 AND 2 PETER 1:5–7

The Marys

SAINTS' DAYS

22 JULY
Mary of Magdala

22 OCTOBER
Mary, the Mother of James and John

9 APRIL
Mary, Wife of Cleophas

25 MAY
The Festival of the Three Marys

29 JUNE
Mary, the Mother of John Mark

There are a number of women in the Bible named Mary: Jesus' mother, Mary; Mary of Magdala (sometimes known as Mary Magdalene), who became the first person to see the risen Jesus; Mary, the mother of James and John, who was present when Jesus was crucified and buried; Mary, the mother of John Mark, who was among the women who helped Jesus and his followers; and Mary, wife of Cleophas, described in the Bible as "the other Mary".

It was confusing – there were at least four Marys. They'd known Jesus when he was at home in Galilee. They'd heard him teach and seen him cure people who were ill. Along with his twelve disciples and several other women, they'd followed him south to Jerusalem.

They'd been with Jesus when he rode into the city seated on a donkey. They'd been there at the cross when he was crucified. Unlike some of the men who'd run away, they'd stayed watching so that Jesus would know he was not alone.

The following Sunday morning, two of them had gone to the tomb where Jesus had been buried. They were among the first to understand that Jesus had come back to life.

But who were they? First was Jesus' mother, Mary, who stayed with him to the very end. Then there was a group sometimes referred to as the Three Marys.

THE THREE MARYS

THIS GROUP OF three women all named Mary included Mary from Magdala, sometimes known as Mary Magdalene. She was one of Jesus' closest friends and was the first person to see Jesus after he rose from the dead on the first Easter morning.

Second was Mary, the mother of the disciples James and John. The Bible says that they were the sons of Zebedee, so she must have been Zebedee's wife. Matthew's Gospel says that she was with Mary from Magdala when Jesus first appeared on Easter morning. She is sometimes known as Saint Mary Salome but she has nothing to do with the other Salome in the Bible who caused the death of John the Baptist.

The third of the Three Marys was Mary, the wife of Cleophas. She too came from Galilee. John, in his Gospel, tells us that she was there with the others when Jesus was crucified. She is also said to be the mother of the disciple known as James the Less.

MARY, THE MOTHER OF
JOHN MARK

THERE IS YET another Mary in the Bible: Mary, the mother of Mark who journeyed with Paul and who later wrote about Jesus in the Gospel of Mark. This Mary is mentioned in the part of the Bible known as the Acts of the Apostles, which describes what happened to the followers of Jesus after he went back to heaven.

One thing that happened was that Peter was put in prison. This was because the authorities didn't like what he'd been saying about Jesus.

One night, he suddenly found the prison gates were unlocked. So what did he do? He looked for his friends! There was only one place they could be. "The house of Mary, the mother of John Mark."

And that's where he found them. It was probably in an upper (or upstairs) room in her house in Jerusalem that the followers of Jesus first met in secret to pray together. Many people say that this was the same upper room where Jesus and his twelve disciples had met to have their last supper together the night before he was crucified.

Thomas

Saint's Day

3 July

Thomas was one of Jesus' twelve disciples and is often referred to as "Doubting Thomas". In 1946, a group of Egyptian workmen discovered a number of ancient scrolls. Among them was the Gospel according to Thomas, listing many sayings of Jesus. Some are like the ones in the New Testament Gospels, but it is not certain whether the others are genuine.

JUST AS SOME people always get known by their nicknames, so this disciple of Jesus was always known as the Twin (although we do not know who his twin brother or sister was).

Nowadays, he is known as Thomas, but "Thomas" is simply Aramaic for "twin". Although the Bible says he had another name, Didymus, that word is simply Greek for "twin". Later, he got another nickname – Doubting Thomas.

The Sunday morning after Jesus was crucified, Jesus appeared to Mary from Magdala and one of the other Marys. That evening, Jesus appeared again. This time, most of the other disciples were there. But not Thomas. When he was told about it, he didn't believe what had happened. How could anyone come back from the dead?

"Unless I see the marks of the nails in his hands," he said, "I won't believe it. Unless I put my hand on those marks and on the mark where the sword pierced his side, I won't believe."

A week later, the disciples were together again, and this time, Thomas was with them. The door was locked, but suddenly, Jesus was standing among them. "Thomas," he said, "put your finger here and see my hands, and put your hand on my side. Stop doubting and believe!"

Thomas replied, "My Lord and my God."

From then on, he believed that Jesus had come back from the dead.

Not much else is said about him in the Bible. But there is another story about Thomas. It tells how the twelve disciples drew lots to decide which countries they should visit in order to tell people about Jesus. It fell to Thomas to go to India. He didn't like this idea, and it so happened that a merchant named Abban was looking for a carpenter to help build a new palace for his king, Gundafor, who was king of Parthia (in what is now Iran). Thomas was a carpenter and decided to go to Parthia instead.

King Gundafor gave him a great deal of money to pay for the new palace and then went on his travels. When he returned, he found Thomas had given the money to the poor and had spent his time preaching and teaching people the message of

Jesus. Gundafor put him in prison and threatened to put him to death.

Before that could happen, the king's brother was taken ill – so ill that everyone thought he was dying. Instead, he recovered and immediately told Gundafor not to kill Thomas. "When I was ill, I was taken to heaven by angels and I was shown a palace more wonderful than any on earth. And I was told such joys are waiting in heaven for all those who believe the Christian message."

King Gundafor was so impressed he sent a message that Thomas should be released from prison and should come to tell him about Jesus. Thomas did, and King Gundafor and his brother both became Christians. It is said that Thomas then journeyed on to India.

Jesus said:
"Blessed are the poor for yours is the kingdom
of heaven."

Jesus said:
"I am the All…
Split wood, I am there.
Lift up the stone and you will find me there."

SAYINGS FROM THE GOSPEL OF THOMAS

Stephen

SAINT'S DAY

26 DECEMBER

Stephen was the first follower of Jesus to lose his life because of what he believed – the first Christian martyr. Because of this, his saint's day is the very first day after Jesus' own birthday.

W HY DIDN'T HE just keep quiet? He was intelligent. He must have known what would happen if he spoke out. He'd be put to death by stoning. But Stephen knew that he must say what he believed was the truth.

A year or so after Jesus had risen from the dead, the Bible says that the twelve apostles (Jesus' special disciples) had chosen seven men to be deacons. Their job was to look after any of the new followers of Jesus who were in need – such as children whose parents had died, or widows who had no one to look after them. This meant that the apostles themselves had time to concentrate on spreading the word of Jesus.

Stephen was one of those seven deacons. He was a tall, energetic young man who also found time to teach and heal many people. He was particularly successful at persuading Jews to join the followers of Jesus – a group that was beginning to be known as "the Church".

Not surprisingly, the members of the Jewish council were not pleased. They paid a number of men to tell lies about Stephen. These men agreed to say such things as, "We heard Stephen speaking against God," and "We heard him say that the Temple should be torn down and everything about our religion should be changed." Having got this so-called evidence, the members of the council had Stephen arrested and brought to trial.

"You've heard the evidence against you," they said. "What have you got to say for yourself?"

Stephen began to speak, clearly and confidently. He told them the story of the Jewish people, of how they had been guided and helped by God, and how God had used a man named Moses to lead them out of Egypt when they had been slaves in that country. It was a story they all knew very well. And Stephen went on to tell how God had sent prophets, or teachers, who had explained his will for his people.

But then Stephen reminded them how they had not always listened to the prophets and had even killed some of them. Then he said the thing that was to cause all the trouble: "Just as you killed God's prophets in days gone by, so now you have betrayed and killed God's own Son, Jesus. You have murdered him!"

The members of the council blocked their ears. "Blasphemy!" they shouted. By blasphemy, they meant he was saying something about God that was untrue because they did not believe that Jesus was God's Son.

The punishment for blasphemy was stoning. They seized Stephen and dragged him from the building, along the streets, and out through the city wall. The men who'd given false evidence against Stephen took off their cloaks and gave them to a young man named Saul to look after. Then they picked up stones and rocks and started pelting Stephen.

Stephen knelt down and prayed as the stones began to hit him: "Lord Jesus, receive my spirit into heaven, and do not hold my death against these men." Soon he was lying on the ground, covered in blood. The men kept on throwing stones until they were sure he was dead.

Saul, who was a Jewish rabbi, watched the execution. He thought that what they had done was a good thing. He was well educated and he knew the law. In his eyes, Stephen had committed blasphemy and so deserved to die. But Saul would later change his mind.

Paul

SAINT'S DAYS

25 JANUARY
Conversion of Paul

29 JUNE

Paul was a Jew from Tarsus, in Cilicia (now part of
southern Turkey), and he worked as a tent maker. He
was a Pharisee, like his father, and studied the Law,
but was also a free "citizen" of the Roman empire.
This gave him legal protection and other rights.
After becoming a believer in Jesus, Paul undertook
many journeys outside Palestine and began the task of
making Christianity a worldwide faith. He preached
to Jews and non-Jews ("Gentiles") on his travels and is
often known as the Apostle to the Gentiles.

IT WAS THE stoning of Stephen that started it. Saul
had watched it happen and it made up his mind.
The followers of Jesus were dangerous. They must
be destroyed.

That very day he started going from house to
house in Jerusalem, determined to discover all
those who believed in Jesus. He dragged them out
of their homes and had them thrown into prison.

The law was on Saul's side. According to the
Jewish authorities, anyone who believed that Jesus
was the Son of God and had risen from the dead
was guilty of blasphemy. The punishment for this
was death.

Despite this, the Christian belief was spreading.
In particular, there was a large number of followers
of Jesus in Damascus. So Saul went to the high

priest of the Jews in Jerusalem and asked for permission to arrest these people and bring them back to Jerusalem for trial. Then he set off on the long and dangerous journey.

Suddenly, as he was nearing the city of Damascus, lightning seemed to flash all around him and he fell to the ground. He heard a voice: "Saul, Saul, why do you persecute me?"

"Who are you?" Saul asked fearfully.

"I am Jesus," he heard the voice say. "I am Jesus, whom you persecute. Now get up and go to Damascus. You'll be told what to do."

The men who were journeying with Saul stood there uncertainly. They'd heard the voice but seen no one. It was as Saul staggered to his feet that he realized he could see nothing. He was blind.

His companions took him to the house of a man named Judas who lived on Straight Street in the middle of Damascus. Saul stayed there for three days, unable to see and refusing food and drink.

At this time, a Christian in Damascus named Ananias had a vision. God spoke to him, telling him to go to Straight Street and ask for Saul at the house of Judas. But Ananias was afraid, for he had heard all about Saul and what he'd done in Jerusalem.

"Don't worry," said the voice of God. "Saul's been praying. He knows you're coming."

Ananias visited Saul, put his hands on his head, and told him that Jesus had sent him so that Saul might see again and believe. And from that moment, Saul's sight returned. He was baptized as a Christian and began to preach in Damascus, praising Jesus as the Son of God.

Not surprisingly, Saul was now mistrusted by both Jews and the followers of Jesus. Eventually, he had to escape during the night by being lowered in a basket from the city walls. From then on, Saul became known by his Roman name, Paul.

Paul returned to Jerusalem but the followers of Jesus there were highly suspicious of him. Wasn't this the man they knew as Saul? Saul, who had stood by, watching Stephen being stoned to death? Saul, who'd had so many of their friends thrown into prison?

At last, Barnabas spoke up for him. He'd heard what had happened to Saul on the way to Damascus. So Saul (or Paul) stayed there, preaching the message of Jesus. This annoyed some of his old friends. Soon his life was in danger again, so he went home to Tarsus.

It's likely that he spent the next ten years teaching and carrying on his trade of tent making. Then, around the year 45, a group of Christians in

Antioch decided that the message of Jesus should be spread to other countries. They chose Paul and Barnabas to do this work.

They took a man named John Mark with them too and sailed to the island of Cyprus and then on to Asia Minor (now southern Turkey). John Mark then returned to Jerusalem, but Barnabas and Paul continued their travels for another year.

Paul made two more great journeys. His next one took him again through Asia Minor, and then, for the first time, he visited Europe, preaching in the Greek cities of Thessalonica, Athens, and Corinth.

His third journey took him back to a city named Ephesus, then again to Thessalonica and Corinth, and eventually back to Jerusalem.

On these journeys, he visited old friends and made new ones. He also kept in touch with people who had become Christians. He did this by writing letters to them. For example, while he was in Corinth, he wrote to the Christians in Thessalonica, and when he was in Ephesus, he wrote to the Christians in Corinth.

He had many adventures on his journeys. When Paul was on his first journey with Barnabas, he visited a place named Lystra. In the crowd, there was a man who had been lame since birth. As he was listening to Paul, Paul turned to him and said, "Stand up straight!" The man stood up and started walking. He'd been healed!

On his second journey, while he was in a town named Philippi, Paul met a slave girl who was troubled by an evil spirit. This spirit allowed her to tell people's fortunes and in this way, she earned a lot of money for her owners. Paul cured her. This infuriated her owners. They seized Paul and his companion Silas and had them thrown into prison.

While they were locked up, an earthquake destroyed all the prison doors. Instead of escaping, Paul and Silas told the prison guard about Jesus, and the guard and his family were baptized.

After his third journey, Paul returned to Jerusalem. Naturally, many local people recognized him and started talking among themselves.

"You know who that is? Paul! Used to be named Saul."

"He's the one who lets the heathen come into our places of worship."

"Everywhere he goes, he persuades Jews to forget about Moses and the prophets and gets them to worship that Jesus."

This wasn't true, but within a few minutes the crowd had become an angry mob. They turned on

Paul and dragged him out of the Temple, where he had gone to worship, and set on him. The commander of the Roman troops in the city heard what was going on and quickly took some officers and soldiers down to where the trouble was.

Paul was put in prison, partly for his own safety, partly because the Romans didn't properly understand why the Jews were accusing him. After about two years, Paul demanded (as was his right as a Roman citizen) to be sent to Rome and tried before the emperor.

In about the year 60, Paul was sent by ship with some other prisoners to Rome. His friend Luke went with him. It was autumn and the Mediterranean Sea was rough. The captain refused to take Paul's advice to take shelter on the island of Crete, and a violent storm blew them westward for over a fortnight.

Then, one daybreak, they finally saw land. When they reached the shore, they discovered they were on the island of Malta. They were given a warm welcome and Paul healed many sick people on the island.

Three months later, they sailed on another ship to Italy and went by road to Rome. Once in Rome, Paul was able to rent an ordinary house and live in it, but he was still under arrest and had a soldier to guard him. He was allowed visitors, and many Jews came to hear him teach. He also spent much of his time writing letters to Christians in places he'd visited on his earlier journeys. This went on for two years.

It's uncertain what happened next. He may have been put on trial, or he may have been allowed to undertake more travels. Many people believe that he was finally put to death sometime between the years 64 and 67. As a Roman citizen, he would have been executed quickly rather than suffering a painful slow death by crucifixion.

Thanks to Paul, the Christian faith had reached the great city of Rome, the heart of the mighty Roman empire.

Barnaby, Timothy, and Titus

SAINTS' DAYS

11 JUNE
Barnabas

26 JANUARY
Timothy

26 JANUARY
Titus

Paul had a number of good friends who accompanied him on his journeys. One of these was Barnabas, who introduced Paul to the apostles of Jesus. He was also the founder of the church in Cyprus. Another was Timothy, one of Paul's most trusted followers. In the Bible, there are two of Paul's epistles (or letters) to Timothy, although it is unlikely that they were written by Paul himself. Yet another friend was Titus, who became a bishop on the island of Crete.

BARNABAS

IT WASN'T EASY being followers of Jesus. Everyone seemed to be against them – the Jews, the Romans...

But there was one person who always managed to cheer them up. Joseph was a Jew, born on the island of Cyprus, who had come to Jerusalem when Jesus was still teaching and preaching. His nickname was "Barnabas", which means "the one who encourages" in Hebrew or Aramaic.

He was also generous. Soon after Stephen was stoned to death, Barnabas sold a field he owned and gave the money to the apostles to help any of Jesus' followers who were in need. He was the first person in Jerusalem to trust Paul after his return from Damascus.

Some time later, Barnabas went to Antioch – the

first place where the followers of Jesus were known as Christians. The Christians there were deciding who should travel around the Mediterranean Sea to tell people about Jesus. Paul was one choice, Barnabas was the other. Young John Mark also joined them for the start of their voyage.

It was on this journey that Paul and Barnabas visited Lystra. The people thought that Barnabas was Zeus, the king of the Greek gods, so he was probably tall and handsome.

Barnabas faithfully accompanied Paul for the whole of that first journey. Sadly, they didn't remain good friends. Their quarrel happened when Paul was planning his second journey. Barnabas wanted to take John Mark with them again.

"No," Paul said firmly. "He only came part way on our first journey. Then he went home. He doesn't get a second chance."

Paul took Silas with him instead, while Barnabas went home to Cyprus with John Mark.

TIMOTHY

ON PAUL'S SECOND journey, he visited Lystra again. He met a Jewish woman named Eunice. She was married to a Greek man, and they had a grown-up son named Timothy. The whole family became Christians, and Timothy joined Paul and Silas on the rest of their journey.

Paul trusted Timothy to travel on his own to teach other Christians about Jesus. Timothy visited Thessalonica, Corinth, and Philippi, among other places. Later, Paul sent him to live in Ephesus.

Paul had visited Ephesus twice himself. There was a temple there where local people went to worship the goddess Artemis (sometimes known as Diana). When Paul persuaded many people to worship Jesus, he caused trouble among the people who sold Artemis souvenirs.

Timothy became the leader, or bishop, of the Christians in Ephesus but, it is said, was killed there in the year 97 when he also preached that it was wrong to worship Artemis.

TITUS

TITUS WAS ANOTHER young Christian friend of Paul's. After Paul had visited Corinth on his second journey, he sent Titus there to be his spokesman. Later, Paul sent Titus to be leader, or bishop, of the church on the island of Crete. Titus lived and worked there until his death in the year 96.

John Mark
and Luke

SAINTS' DAYS

25 APRIL
John Mark

18 OCTOBER
Luke

*In the Bible, there are four retellings of the life of Jesus
– the four Gospels. These include the Gospel of Mark
(thought to be the first Gospel to be written) and the
Gospel of Luke. The writer of Mark is believed to be
John Mark, a young man who became a close friend of
the disciples. In paintings, he is often shown dressed as
a bishop and holding a pen. The Gospel of Luke was
probably written by a doctor named Luke, one of the
first non-Jewish followers of Jesus.*

JOHN MARK

IT WAS VERY embarrassing. John Mark had run
through the streets with no clothes on. He only
hoped no one had seen.

It had all started earlier in the week, when
two men had come to his mother's house. They
had made arrangements for a special meal in an
upstairs room.

Then a man named Jesus and his twelve
friends came to have supper there. Very late at
night, they left. Curious, John Mark slipped out
of bed to follow them, just wrapping a linen sheet
around himself. They went to a garden known as
Gethsemane, and he hid in the shadows, watching
to see what would happen.

Sometime after midnight, the high priest's
guards came along with one of the men who'd had

supper in the upper room. That man kissed Jesus, and then the guards arrested Jesus. After a scuffle, Jesus' friends ran away. In the confusion, the guards caught John Mark. But the sheet slipped off, and he was able to dash away in the darkness.

Over the next few days, Jesus' friends used the upstairs room as a secret meeting place. John Mark learned about Jesus and became a close friend of a disciple named Peter.

In time, John Mark himself became a follower of Jesus. Several years later, he set off on a long journey with Barnabas and Paul, to places such as Cyprus and Asia Minor, to tell people about Jesus.

After a while, John Mark returned to Jerusalem. This annoyed Paul, but years later, when Paul was being kept under arrest in Rome, he asked Timothy to arrange for John Mark to go to Rome to help him.

About this time, Peter also went to Rome. He preached openly about Jesus, and the large crowds who came to listen persuaded John Mark to write everything down. It seems that John Mark did this and made copies of this "Gospel" for all who wanted.

Later, John Mark went to Alexandria in Egypt to teach people about Jesus. He died there, probably in about the year 68. It is said that his body was later taken to the city of Venice in what is now Italy.

LUKE

NOT MUCH IS known about Luke except that he spoke Greek, he was a doctor, and he was a great friend of Paul. He decided to travel with Paul on his journey to Rome and stayed there with him while Paul was under house arrest. During this time, it is likely that he wrote the Acts of the Apostles, the book that tells the stories of the early Christians, including Paul.

It is evident from Luke's Gospel that he was a kind man. He makes special mention of the many times that Jesus cared for the poor and the outcast. He also makes clear that Jesus respected women as much as men.

It is believed that Luke died at the age of eighty-four some time before the end of the first century.

Clement and Ignatius of Antioch

23 NOVEMBER
Clement

17 OCTOBER
Ignatius of Antioch

As the years went by, the people who had known
Jesus and his friends grew older and began to die.
Some were put to death because of what they
believed and taught. That meant that the various
groups of Christians in different places around the
Mediterranean Sea needed new leaders or "bishops".
The first bishops were chosen by the original apostles
(and Peter himself was the first bishop of Rome), and
then they chose the leaders who were to become bishops
after them. Clement and Ignatius were two bishops in
the early Christian church.

CLEMENT

IN ONE OF his letters, Paul says that one of his
helpers was a man named Clement. Clement
was originally a slave and also probably a Jew, but
he later became a Christian. Eventually, he became
bishop of Rome.

During the ten years that he was bishop,
Clement wrote a "long and wonderful" letter to the
Christians at Corinth in the year 95. The Epistle of
Clement was not included in the New Testament,
even though it is older than some of the books that
are included.

The Christians at Corinth had been arguing
among themselves about various matters, and in his
epistle, Clement sent them lots of advice:

The strong must make sure they care for the weak.
The rich must be certain to give enough to supply
all the needs of the poor.
The poor must thank God for supplying their needs.
We all need each other: the great need the small;
the small need the great.
In our body, the head is useless without the feet
and the feet without the head.
The tiniest limbs of our body are useful
and necessary to the whole.

This letter was read aloud in the churches in
Corinth for many years.

It is not certain how or when Clement died,
but it was probably in about the year 101. There
is a story that suggests he was sentenced to work
in slave-like conditions and was later put to death
by being thrown into the sea with an anchor tied
to his neck. Clement is therefore often linked with
the sea, and seaside churches are sometimes named
after him for this reason.

It is said that several hundred years after his
death, Clement's body was recovered and buried
in Rome in the place that was his home, where the
Church of San Clemente now stands.

IGNATIUS OF ANTIOCH

THE BIBLE SAYS that one day, the disciples of Jesus were arguing among themselves about which of them was the greatest. Jesus wanted to teach them not to be proud. He took a young boy and placed him in front of them. "The greatest person is the one who humbles himself and becomes like this child."

Some people believe that boy grew up to become Bishop Ignatius of Antioch, the town in Syria from where Paul and Barnabas started their first great journey. It is at least very likely that Ignatius knew and was a disciple of the apostle John.

Ignatius became bishop in about the year 60 and was leader of the Christians in Antioch for forty years. He was then condemned to death by the Romans and sent by ship to Rome. During that journey, he wrote seven letters to Christians in different places to encourage them to trust in Jesus.

Ignatius was killed in about the year 101 by being thrown to the lions, probably in the arena in Rome known as the Colosseum.

Lawrence, Valentine, and Sebastian

SAINTS' DAYS

10 AUGUST
Lawrence

14 FEBRUARY
Valentine

20 JANUARY
Sebastian

For much of the two hundred years following the life
of Jesus, the Romans allowed Christians (and others)
to worship as they wished. Then, in the year 249,
Decius became ruler of the Roman empire. He wanted
everyone to worship the old gods of Rome. Many
Christians refused. They were tortured and executed.
Decius was killed in 251, but many of the emperors
after him were equally cruel. Lawrence, Valentine,
and Sebastian were all put to death as a result of their
Christian beliefs and for teaching people about Jesus.

LAWRENCE

LAWRENCE WAS HEARTBROKEN. His hero, Pope Sixtus, was about to be put to death. Was there nothing he could do to save this man whom he admired and served?

Lawrence was one of the deacons of the Christian church in Rome. As deacon, Lawrence was in charge of the church's money.

The year was 258, and the emperor had tried to make Pope Sixtus worship the Roman gods. He'd refused, and that was why he'd been arrested, tortured, and was now being taken away for execution. Lawrence followed, noisily demanding to know why the pope was being murdered and his deacon left alive. Pope Sixtus warned Lawrence that he too would be put to death in three days' time.

On hearing this, Lawrence gave away everything he owned to the poor, the hungry, and the orphans and widows of the city. He even sold some of the church's gold and silver to help the needy. News of this got about, and Lawrence was seized and taken to a Roman officer known as the prefect.

The prefect ordered Lawrence to produce the remaining money and any treasures the church owned (such as gold candlesticks or cups) and hand them over.

Lawrence thought quickly. "If you give me three days to organize it, I'll bring you the church's treasure."

During the next three days, he gathered together all the disabled people and beggars, together with many blind and sick people and hundreds of lepers. He led them to the prefect.

"Here," said Lawrence. "These people are the true treasures of the church. You see, the church is far, far richer than your emperor."

The prefect was not amused. It is said that he ordered his men to put Lawrence to death in a slow and horrible way. They produced an iron grid and lit a fire underneath it. When the iron grid began to glow in the heat, they bound Lawrence to it with chains so that he would roast to death.

Even then, Lawrence's clever wit did not desert

him. It is reported that after a while he said, "You can turn me over now. I'm done on that side."

As he neared death, he prayed that Rome would become a Christian city. This did indeed happen, but not for another hundred years.

The story of Lawrence's gruesome end may not be entirely accurate (it is more likely that he was executed according to the Roman law of the time), but he is remembered as a martyr around the world. A river in Canada, a cathedral in Spain, and many churches are all named after him. He is also the patron saint of cooks!

VALENTINE

EVERYONE HAS HEARD about Saint Valentine. He's the patron saint of lovers, and on his day, people send anonymous cards or presents to the one they love. But who was he?

Well, there was a priest named Valentine who lived in Rome in the third century. He was put in prison because he helped some Christians who were going to be executed by a cruel emperor named Claudius.

While Valentine was in prison, he healed the chief warder's daughter, who was blind, and the warder and all his family became Christians.

When Emperor Claudius heard this, he said that Valentine should be executed.

And so, on 14 February in the year 269, Valentine was clubbed to death. Then his head was chopped off, just to make sure he was dead.

In the same year, another man named Valentine, who was the bishop of Terni (about sixty miles from Rome), was also put to death by Emperor Claudius for being a Christian.

Neither saint seems to have anything to do with young lovers. No one knows the reason why the modern customs linked to Valentine's Day began in England and France in the Middle Ages.

Some say it was because on this day of the year (in the northern hemisphere) birds pair up and start mating. Others say the day is special for lovers because at that time of year there had been a pagan Roman festival named Lupercalia, when young men took part in a kind of lottery to find a partner. But Lupercalia has nothing to do with either Saint Valentine!

SEBASTIAN

SEBASTIAN WAS THE son of a nobleman. He was born in France but brought up in Italy, in Milan, the hometown of his parents. Although Sebastian was a Christian, he joined the Roman army in the year 283. He kept his beliefs secret because he thought he could do more good as a Christian spy inside the army!

Some Christians who knew the truth about Sebastian brought a woman named Zoe to him. She had lost the power of speech. Sebastian prayed with her and she quickly recovered. As a result, many people who knew her became Christians.

About the same time, a new emperor, Emperor Diocletian, promoted Sebastian to be captain of the Praetorian Guard, a regiment that acted as the emperor's very own bodyguard. Diocletian, who hated all Christians, had no idea that his most trusted officer was leading a double life.

Some time later, the authorities discovered that Zoe and some of her friends were Christians. They were arrested and sentenced to death. Some were drowned; others were buried alive or beheaded. Diocletian believed that the Christians were a threat to the security of the empire. Even the pope had to go into hiding.

It was too much for Sebastian. He went to see the emperor, announced that he was a Christian too, and told the emperor what he thought of his cruelty. Diocletian was furious. He ordered that Sebastian be put to death in a terrible way.

Sebastian was stripped and tied to a tree. His

fellow officers were then ordered to use him as a target for archery practice. Arrow after arrow was shot into his body, and Sebastian was left for dead.

A Christian widow named Irene came to rescue his body and was amazed to discover that Sebastian was still just alive. She cared for his many wounds and nursed him back to health.

As soon as he had recovered, Sebastian went and hid in a passageway he knew the emperor walked along regularly. As Diocletian approached, Sebastian stepped out and once again told him what he thought of his cruelty.

Diocletian could say nothing for a moment because he was so shocked at seeing the man he was sure had been shot to death. But as soon as he recovered, he again ordered Sebastian to be put to death. This time Sebastian was beaten to death with heavy clubs and his body was thrown into one of the city's sewers.

Although Sebastian and others suffered such immense cruelty for their faith, they would surely have been encouraged by words such as these:

Even if you should suffer for doing what is right,
how happy you are! Do not be afraid of anyone,
and do not worry. But have reverence for Christ
in your hearts, and honour him as Lord.

Be ready at all times to answer anyone who asks you to explain the hope you have in you, but do it with gentleness and respect. Keep your conscience clear, so that when you are insulted, those who speak evil of your good conduct as followers of Christ will be ashamed of what they say.

Be alert, be on the watch! Your enemy, the Devil, roams round like a roaring lion, looking for someone to devour. Be firm in your faith and resist him, because you know that your fellow-believers in all the world are going through the same kind of sufferings. But after you have suffered for a little while, the God of all grace, who calls you to share his eternal glory in union with Christ, will himself perfect you and give you firmness, strength, and a sure foundation. To him be the power for ever! Amen.

1 PETER 3:14–16 AND 5:8–11

George

Saint's Day

23 APRIL

Many stories have been told about Saint George,
including the story of George and the dragon. Yet
all we know is that there was a Roman centurion,
or tribune, named George from Cappadocia, who
became a Christian and was consequently put to death
in about the year 300. Because he wasn't afraid to say
he was a Christian, he was later made a saint. When
English soldiers were fighting in Palestine in battles
known as the Crusades, they adopted him as their
protector, and in 1212, George became the patron saint
of England. He is also a patron saint of Portugal and
of many other places.

O NCE UPON A time, there lived a huge and
terrible dragon. Its home was in a large lake
near a distant city. Whenever it was hungry, it
would come out of the lake and seize any sheep
it could find in the area and greedily eat them up
before lumbering back into the lake.

The people tried attacking the dragon, but it
simply snorted fire from its giant nostrils, driving
them back in terror and filling the air with its
deadly polluting breath. Many of the people
became ill and died from the pollution alone.
Because of this, the city was always gloomy and
sad.

Finally, the people went to their king and asked,

"What can we do? Soon we'll all have perished because of that dragon!"

"If we sacrifice one of our daughters down by the lake each day, that would at least keep it away from the city," suggested the king. "We could draw lots to see who is to be sacrificed each day." Sensing that the crowd wasn't too keen on this idea, the king added, "Although I've only got one daughter, she must take her chance as well."

Nobody had a better idea, so they decided to follow the king's advice.

Every day, a family gave up one of their daughters to be a meal for the dragon. Before long, it fell to the royal family to sacrifice their daughter, Cleodolinda.

As she was led out, the king watched her go with tears in his eyes. She stood on the shore of the lake, sobbing bitterly. But as she did so, who should ride up on a white horse but a handsome young man dressed in a Roman officer's uniform!

"What's the matter?" he asked.

"Kind sir, whoever you are," replied Cleodolinda, "ride away from here!"

"My name is George," said the man, "and I won't leave until you tell me why you're here."

So she told him about the dragon. Just as she finished her story, with a roar and with its usual amount of splashing, the dragon emerged from the lake.

George made the sign of the cross on himself and said the words, "In the name of the Father, and the Son, and the Holy Spirit." Then he charged on his horse at the dragon. He thrust his spear with all his strength into its throat, pinned the animal to the earth, and his horse then trampled the dragon under its feet.

Once it was docile, George ordered Cleodolinda to tie the white belt she was wearing around the dragon's neck and lead it into the city, like a dog on a leash. Nervously, she did.

When they saw this extraordinary procession, the people were astonished. And afraid.

"Don't be afraid, but trust in the Lord Jesus Christ," said George, "for it was he who sent me to you to save you from the dragon."

Then he killed the dragon. The people dragged the carcass out of the city and burned it. Fifteen thousand of them became Christians.

Christopher

SAINT'S DAY

25 JULY

There is little evidence to indicate when Christopher lived, or even if he existed. As a result, his name was removed from the official list of Roman Catholic saints in 1969. However, he is still considered to be the patron saint of those on journeys, and people sometimes say the words "Saint Christopher protect" as a prayer before setting off. According to tradition in the Eastern Church, Christopher was born in Toledo in Spain and lived in the third century. His name in Greek, Christophoros, means "the one who carries Christ".

CHRISTOPHER WAS A giant of a man, so the story goes. He was extremely proud of his size and his strength. And he wanted to serve the most powerful king in the world. So he decided to look for him.

At last, he found an extremely rich and mighty king and happily became his servant.

Then one day, some entertainers arrived at the king's court. They sang songs and ballads to the king and his courtiers. All went well until they sang a song about the devil. Christopher noticed that the king turned pale and started to tremble. The devil must be greater than this king, thought Christopher. That's who I must serve. And off he went to find the devil.

The devil was delighted to have a strong assistant, and Christopher was pleased to be serving someone more powerful than any earthly king.

One day, they were out riding. When they came to a large cross that had been placed at the roadside, the devil took one look at it, shuddered, and galloped off as fast as he could.

"Why did he do that?" asked Christopher.

"That's the sign of Jesus," one of the junior devils replied.

Christopher realized that Jesus must be a greater king than the devil – so off he went in search of Jesus.

Eventually, he met a holy man who told him that the best way to find Jesus was through prayer and by fasting. But Christopher had never learned to pray and did not want to give up food in case it weakened his strength.

"In that case," said the holy man, "you should use the gifts God has given you." And he showed Christopher a deep and dangerous river. It crossed the route that many Christians followed when they were making a journey to the Holy Land, where Jesus had once lived. "You could use your strength to carry these pilgrims on your shoulders across the river," he suggested.

And that is what Christopher did for many years.

One night, he was woken from his sleep by a boy's voice. The child wanted to be carried across the river there and then. "But it's dark and stormy," said Christopher. "Why not wait till morning?"

The boy insisted, so Christopher put him on his shoulders, took up his stout stick, and started to wade through the swirling river.

At first, it seemed easy, but then the child seemed to grow heavier and heavier, and Christopher feared he might stumble. At last, they reached the other side.

"You began to feel very heavy," said Christopher. "It was as if I was carrying the whole world on my shoulders."

"No wonder," said the child, "for I am Jesus, who saved the world from sin by taking the weight of all the sins of the world upon me."

"I don't believe that!" replied Christopher.

"Plant your stick in the ground. Tomorrow it will be bearing flowers and fruit at the same time. That will prove that you have indeed found the one you should serve."

And the next morning, the stick had become a tree bearing both flowers and fruit, and Christopher had indeed found the greatest king of all.

Catherine of Alexandria

Saint's Day

25 November

Nothing can be proved about the life of Catherine,
and there is real doubt about whether she ever lived.
If she did exist, then she must have died in the year
306 or 307, which was when Maxentius was ruler of
the Roman empire. Despite these uncertainties, she
was a most popular saint during the Middle Ages,
but because many of the stories told about her are so
unlikely, her name was removed from the official list
of Roman Catholic saints in 1969.

S HE WAS ABOUT eighteen and her name was
Catherine. She lived in the Egyptian city of
Alexandria.

Catherine lived during the reign of the Roman
emperor Maxentius and was famous throughout
the city for her beauty. Despite this, she was the sort
of person who liked to spend her time reading and
studying. Indeed, she was just as famous for her
intelligence as she was for her good looks.

Now it so happened that Emperor Maxentius
made a visit to Alexandria, which was part
of his empire. While he was there, he heard
about Catherine's beauty and intelligence. He
commanded his servants to bring her to meet him.
As soon as he saw her, he decided he wanted to
marry her. Immediately. But there was a problem.
Maxentius already had a wife.

Maxentius (who continued to worship the ancient Roman gods) didn't think this mattered at all.

"Oh, don't worry," he said. "I'll have two wives at the same time. I'm the emperor, I can do what I like."

Catherine was having none of this. She refused his proposal, saying that as a Christian she couldn't possibly agree to such a relationship.

Maxentius then gathered together a great number of teachers and professors who also believed in the Roman gods. He told them to persuade Catherine that her Christian faith was nonsense. She listened to them for a while and then started answering their points convincingly and persuasively. The result was that, far from getting Catherine to change her mind, these wise men began to change their own minds.

The emperor was not only angry; he was alarmed. What would happen if Rome gave up its worship of the old gods? He didn't want any of what he described as "this Christian nonsense".

So he gave orders that Catherine should be put to death in a particularly horrible way. He had a large wheel made, with sharp blades set into the outside rim. Then Catherine was to be tied around this edge, and the blades were intended to cut her to pieces as the wheel was rolled along.

It didn't go according to plan. When Catherine was bound to the wheel, it broke and the blades flew off in all directions, flashing in the light and wounding the soldiers who were supposed to be putting her to death. Some people say all this was caused by lightning striking the wheel. Whether that is true or not, Catherine's executioners didn't try making another wheel. They beheaded her at once.

It is said that a flight of angels then descended from heaven and carried her body to Mount Sinai, where, centuries before, God had given the Ten Commandments to Moses. Even today there is a monastery named Saint Catherine's there.

People also remember the death of Saint Catherine with the firework that is named after her, which is supposed to spin around as her wheel did.

Constantine
and Helena

Saints' Days

21 MAY
Constantine

18 AUGUST
Helena

The son of Constantius and Helena, Constantine was proclaimed Roman emperor in the year 306. After gaining full control of the empire, he rebuilt the ancient city of Byzantium (now Istanbul), which he renamed Constantinople. Under his rule, Christians were free to practise their beliefs, and in 321, he made Sunday a public holiday so Christians could worship on that day. He himself was baptized shortly before his death in 337. He is so highly thought of in the Eastern Church that he is described there as the Thirteenth Apostle.

It was the day before the battle that he saw the sign. Above the midday sun, shining in the sky, there it was – a cross. There was no mistaking it. It was the sign Christians used to remind themselves of Jesus. And circling it were the Latin words *in hoc signo vinces*, meaning "By this sign, you shall conquer". It was a vision that would change the Roman empire for ever.

CONSTANTINE

THE REASON CONSTANTINE was going to do battle the next day was to decide once and for all who should be ruler of the Roman empire. When his father, Constantius, had died six years earlier, he'd been proclaimed emperor. There was no doubt about that. The problem was that one of his generals, General Maxentius, had other ideas. He thought he should be emperor, and now the matter was going to be settled by a battle close to a bridge that crossed the River Tiber near Rome.

The night before the battle, Constantine had a dream. Jesus appeared to him in the dream and said that he must make the cross his own symbol and have it placed on all the imperial flags and standards. The next morning, 28 October in the year 312, the battle began.

As the army of General Maxentius began to advance across the bridge, it collapsed, flinging many of his soldiers into the river. Constantine won easily.

HELENA

CONSTANTINE'S MOTHER, HELENA, immediately became a Christian. She started using her wealth to help the Christian faith by building new churches.

Constantine did indeed adopt the sign he had seen in the sky to be his emblem. It was not a simple cross but what is known as the "chi-rho" symbol, after the first two letters, X and P (*chi* and *rho*), of the Greek word *Christos* meaning "Christ". From then on, that sign was on every Roman standard.

In that same year, Constantine made it legal to be a Christian. Christians no longer had to meet in secret. After 250 years of persecution, it was safe to be a follower of Jesus anywhere in the Roman empire.

Nicholas

Saint's Day

6 December

Many stories are told about this popular saint. In the Netherlands, Saint Nicholas, known as Sinte Klaas, is said to visit children on his feast day and, if they have been good, to leave them presents. When Dutch people settled in America in what is now New York, they kept up this custom. Other people started to name him Santa Claus, and this is when the stories about Santa Claus, or Father Christmas, began. Nicholas is the patron saint of children, sailors, and pawnbrokers. He is also the patron saint of Russia.

H E WAS WISE, he was kind, and he was a bishop — the bishop of Myra in Asia Minor (now southern Turkey). Nicholas was also rich and generous. Whenever he met a poor man, he would give him money. If the poor man tried to say thank you, Nicholas would become very shy and hurry away.

One day, as Nicholas walked around the town, he overheard three young women talking sadly about what was going to happen to them. Nicholas listened. It seemed they were so poor that nobody would marry them, even though they were very beautiful.

When their father came home, he shared their sorrow. He had no work and no hope of getting any. It seemed he might have to sell his daughters into slavery so that they would survive, or they might even have to earn a living as prostitutes. Nicholas tiptoed away.

That night, while they were all sleeping, Nicholas came secretly to the house and threw a round bag of gold coins in through the window. "This is the best way," he said to himself. "If I give them money in an obvious way, it may embarrass their father. Much better to do it secretly." So Nicholas left as quietly as he could.

Next morning, the father was overjoyed. "Now my eldest daughter has a dowry and can get married." Soon there was a wedding and a great party.

Some time after this, Nicholas was passing the same house. The two younger daughters were still sad because nobody would marry them, and their father was again very full of sorrow. Nicholas went quietly home.

That night, Nicholas came tiptoeing around again and threw a second bag of gold in through the window.

Next morning, the family was overjoyed again. "Now my second daughter can get married!" said the father. And soon there was a second wedding and a second great party.

Some days later, Nicholas was again passing the

same house. The father and his youngest daughter were sitting very sorrowfully at home because there was no money for a third wedding. Nicholas went quietly home.

That night, the father didn't go to sleep. He was wondering who had been leaving such generous presents and he wanted to say thank you. Sure enough, Nicholas came tiptoeing around and was about to throw a third bag of gold in through the window when the father heard him and came to the door. Nicholas tried to run away, but the father caught him by the arm and started to thank him. Nicholas explained that he wanted to help all the daughters but he didn't want anyone to make a fuss over him. Even so, the father tried very hard to thank Nicholas properly. Nicholas replied that he must not thank him but thank God, who had given Nicholas money to use sensibly. At last, the two men gave each other a hug of friendship and then Nicholas went on his way. The third daughter was able to get married, Bishop Nicholas blessed the young couple, and there was a bigger party than ever!

Basil the Great
and
Gregory Nazianzen

SAINTS' DAY

2 JANUARY

Basil was born in the year 330 and became bishop of Caesarea. We know a lot about his life from his letters and sermons, many of which have survived. A good friend of his was the priest Gregory of Nazianzen, who later became a bishop. Both Basil and Gregory became known as "fathers" or founders of the church in eastern Europe, and their lives and teachings have inspired Christians there and in Russia throughout the centuries. Basil's guidelines for his followers (known as the Rule of Saint Basil) are still followed by monks in the Eastern Church.

THEY WERE BOTH brainy. Their names were Basil and Gregory, and they were both born in Caesarea, the capital of an area once known as Cappadocia but which, by this time, was known as Pontus. Both Basil and Gregory came from Christian families (Gregory's father was a bishop) and they went as students to Athens University, where they became best friends.

When he was twenty-six, Basil went home to Caesarea and earned his living as a teacher of public speaking, or what the Romans knew as oratory or rhetoric.

Three years later, he gave up his career and set off on a long journey through Palestine and Egypt to visit Christians who were living as hermits.

Eventually, Basil returned to Pontus and he too began living as a hermit. But others came to join him.

After some time, he was glad this had happened and that he was no longer alone. "God has made us like parts of the body," he said. "Just as one part isn't any use without the others, so we need the help of one another." He went on to say, "It is the duty of Christians to love and serve one another. How can you do that if you live alone? Who will you serve?"

To help them in their daily life, Basil made up rules for himself and his new followers, rules that would stop them from wasting time or living without any purpose. These were as follows: pray regularly; help the poor and the sick; study the Bible; eat only one meal a day (of bread, water, and vegetables); and sleep only till midnight, and then get up to pray. In this way, they became the first Christian monks living an organized communal life in one building. In later years, such groups of monks would come to be known as orders and the places where they lived would come to be known as monasteries.

Basil himself gave up this way of life, however, and became a priest in Pontus. Nevertheless, he still believed in the monastic way of life and started several new monasteries.

In the year 370, everyone wanted him to become bishop of his hometown, Caesarea. Basil didn't feel that was right, but his friend Gregory persuaded him to accept. Once he was bishop, he worked hard and organized the building of a large hospital for the sick and the poor near the city gate. It also had a resting place for those on journeys and dwelling places for those in need. It became known as the Basiliad.

At one stage, Basil became unpopular with the local Roman authorities. They threatened to confiscate all his property, banish him, or even put him to death. Basil replied, "Such threats have no power over me. My only possessions are one ragged coat and some books. As for banishment, I'm simply journeying to heaven, and as for death, well, I am weak, but it's only the first blow that will hurt me. Death will be a merciful release."

Basil died in the year 379 when he was only forty-nine, exhausted by hard work. Gregory died ten years later, in 389.

Martin of Tours

SAINT'S DAY

11 NOVEMBER

Martin was born in around 316 and brought up in Italy, the son of a Roman officer. After spending some time in the army himself, he became a Christian and later a monk. In about 370, he was made bishop of Tours in France. Instead of moving into a bishop's palace, Martin shared his wealth and lived simply like a monk. He wore animal skins and never combed his hair. Until his death in 397, he journeyed throughout France, teaching people to love one another, share what they had, and help those in need.

MARTIN WASN'T REALLY a man; not yet. He was fifteen, strong, fit, and tall. Tall enough to join the Roman army, because this was in the days when the Romans ruled most of Europe.

And joining the army was what Martin was doing in a small town in Italy, not far from where he lived. The army doctor examined him and all the other young men who were hoping to become soldiers. Next an officer asked them questions, making sure they were not runaway criminals or slaves who ought to be at home serving their masters.

Each of the young men had brought with him a letter from someone, recommending him as likely to be a good soldier. Martin handed over his letter. The officer read it. "Most impressive," he said.

"From your father, isn't it?"

"Yes, sir," said Martin.

"Met him once. Very brave soldier. And you're going to be just like him. Excellent."

Martin took the army oath, promising to be a soldier and to be loyal to the Roman empire.

In fact, Martin proved to be a very good soldier. He was reliable and popular. Soon, he was promoted to the rank of officer. Now he also wore a sword and a warm red cloak, and he no longer marched on foot with all the other soldiers. Martin rode on a silver-white horse.

When Martin was eighteen, he and his soldiers were posted to another part of the Roman empire. They were sent to guard the town of Amiens in the north of Gaul, in what's now known as France. Martin and his soldiers weren't too pleased about this, for it was winter and very cold there. But at least Martin had his cloak.

One raw, damp evening, Martin was riding slowly through the town, his soldiers marching behind him, when he saw a beggar. The man was wearing just a few damp, torn rags and was shivering with cold.

Martin pulled up his horse, drew his sword, and with one swift movement, cut his warm red cloak in two. He gave half to the beggar, who could hardly believe his luck. Martin's soldiers were amazed. Had their officer gone mad? Ruining his cloak for a beggar? They tried not to laugh. They couldn't help it. But Martin wasn't angry with them.

"That man was cold. I had a cloak. It was right to share it," he said.

In silence, they marched back to their barracks.

That night, Martin had a dream. He thought he saw Jesus, wearing half a Roman soldier's cloak.

"Look," said Jesus in the dream, "this is the cloak that Martin has shared."

Martin's dream made him determined to become a Christian. He was baptized and so became a follower of Jesus. Now he wanted to leave the army, but a war was beginning against a fierce tribe named the Goths. Martin was immediately accused of being a coward for wanting to run away from the war. When he still refused to fight, he was put in prison. Only at the end of the war was he released and allowed to leave the army and become a Christian.

Augustine of Hippo

Saint's Day

28 AUGUST

Augustine lived from the year 354 to 430 and is one of the most important figures in Christian history. For more than a thousand years, his writings have influenced Christians. Nowadays, many Christians disagree with some of what he wrote, such as his belief that babies who die before they are baptized will go to hell. The city of Saint Augustine in Florida (the oldest city in America) is named after him because the Spanish first landed there on his saint's day.

A s HE HIMSELF admitted, he'd been a naughty young man. Although he had been taught about Jesus by his very holy mother, Monica, Augustine had spent his youth doing all kinds of wrong things. He was rebellious at school, and he was also idle. But he was intelligent.

He'd been born in a small village named Tagaste in what is now Algeria in northern Africa. When he was seventeen, he went to study at Carthage University, and it was here that he gave up Christianity, saying it was nonsense. He also made his girlfriend pregnant. They soon had a son, whom they named Adeodatus.

Despite all this, he did well at his studies and, in time, became a teacher. First, he started a school in Tagaste, but he soon returned to Carthage, where he taught at the university.

It was at this time that he began to think again about the faith his mother had taught him. He knew that the way he was living was wrong, but he was also enjoying it. Much later in his life, he wrote down a prayer he had said at this time: "O Lord God, make me good, but not yet."

From Carthage, Augustine moved on to teach in Rome and later in Milan, where his mother and Adeodatus came to join him.

One day, he was sitting in a garden. Some children were playing nearby and he heard one of them shout out, "Take up and read." He absent-mindedly picked up the nearest thing there was to read. It was a copy of Paul's letter to the Romans. He started reading the words "Let us live honestly; not in revelry and drunkenness, not in lust and dirtiness, not in arguing and jealousy, but in the way of Jesus". These words made him think. How had he been spending his life? Had his mother been right all along?

He went to talk to the bishop of Milan, a holy man named Ambrose. After that, Augustine went to many of the services at which Ambrose spoke.

On the evening before Easter Day in the year 387, Augustine was baptized as a Christian by Ambrose. Four years later, Augustine became a priest.

Augustine then went back to Africa and was soon made bishop of Hippo. This oddly named seaport is now named Annaba and is in Algeria. Thanks to Augustine, the Christian church became very strong in that place.

During the thirty-five years he was bishop of Hippo, he employed men to write down his sermons as he preached them. Copies were made and sent to other bishops and to monasteries.

It is from these many books and from his own life story, which is known as the *Confessions*, that we know so much about the man who came to see that Jesus welcomes all people, including sinners, provided they are prepared to reform and live according to his sayings.

Father,
I am seeking:
I am hesitant and uncertain,
but will you, O God,
watch over each step of mine
and guide me.

A PRAYER BY SAINT AUGUSTINE

Patrick

SAINT'S DAY

17 MARCH

Patrick was born in around the year 390 and was
probably part Welsh and part Roman. For thirty years,
he spread the Christian faith throughout Ireland, the
first country in the West outside the Roman empire
to hear the Christian gospel. During that time,
Patrick established many churches, monasteries, and
schools. He died when he was about seventy years old.
Patrick is patron saint of Ireland and his saint's day is
celebrated by Irish people around the world.

WHEN HE WAS sixteen, Patrick was captured by
pirates. They had come to raid his homeland
of Britain, looking for strong lads they could sell as
slaves in Ireland. Patrick was bought by a local chief
in the west of Ireland and set to work as a herdsman.

Ireland had its own pagan gods, its own laws,
and its own language. To young Patrick, it seemed
a wild and strange place. He'd been brought up as a
Christian, but the faith had never meant very much
to him. But now he began to think more about it
and, in particular, about the belief that God is one
being but also God the Father, God the Son who
came to earth, and God the Spirit who is present at
all times. Christians give this idea of three-in-one
the name "the Trinity".

Not surprisingly, Patrick hated the hard life of
slavery. He eventually managed to escape and made

his way to the coast where he found a ship to take him home to Britain.

It was a stormy voyage and the winds blew the ship off course. When it did reach land, no one on board knew where they were. Their food ran out and they were in danger of starving to death.

"You're a Christian," said one of the sailors to Patrick. "Why don't you pray for food?"

He did. Within minutes, a herd of wild pigs came scuttling past. Patrick was suddenly very popular!

Over the next twenty years, Patrick lived mainly in France and studied to become a priest. Later, he was made a bishop and was sent to Ireland in order to spread the word of Jesus there.

At that time, Ireland was divided into tribal groups, each ruled by a chief. One of the chiefs was also called "high king of Ireland" and he ruled from Tara in County Meath. His name was Laoghaire, which is pronounced "Leary".

One day, as the story goes, High King Laoghaire was celebrating a pagan festival. All the fires and lights were put out. No flame was to be seen anywhere until a burning torch was carried out of the king's palace. But it was at the time of Easter, and Patrick lit an Easter candle as a reminder of how Jesus rose from the dead.

The pagans were very angry and threatened Patrick with death, but he boldly explained to King Laoghaire the meaning of Easter. The king listened and Patrick was allowed to travel through Ireland, teaching about Jesus. It was dangerous work because not all the chiefs were as friendly as Laoghaire. Patrick wrote: "Daily I expect either a violent death or to be robbed and reduced to slavery."

Many other stories are told about Patrick. One tells how Patrick rid Ireland of snakes by saying a prayer, which made them all go into the sea. However, there were probably never any snakes in Ireland in the first place. Much more likely to be true is the story of how he explained the Trinity.

"The Trinity is like this shamrock," he explained. "Like the leaf, it's three-in-one. It's only one leaf, but three parts make the complete leaf."

And that, it's said, is why the shamrock became the emblem of Ireland.

Brigid

Saint's Day

1 FEBRUARY

*Brigid (also known as Bridget or Bride) is thought to
have lived from about 450 until 523. Not many facts
are known about her, but there are numerous stories.
It is said that one rainy day, she came home and threw
her wet cloak over a beam of sunlight to dry, mistaking
it for a wooden rail. The cloak stayed hanging in
mid-air on the ray of sunlight, until long after the sun
had set. Brigid is one of Ireland's patron saints and is
sometimes known as "the Mary of Ireland".*

ONE OF THE good things about Brigid was
that she was very generous. She was always
ready to give anything she had to other people. The
problem was that she sometimes gave away things
that weren't really hers to give.

Brigid was the daughter of an Irish chief and one
of his maids. While she was still a child, her father
sold her as a slave girl to another chief. This chief
set her to work in his dairy, where the milk from
his cows was made into butter and cheese. One
day a great number of poor people came begging
for food. Brigid was so sorry for them that she gave
away almost all the cheese and butter on the dairy
shelves.

When she was about thirteen years old, her
father brought her home to work for him. She still
couldn't help giving things away if anyone was in

need. Clothes, pots and pans, food – she gave them all to those who had none.

It wasn't long before her father decided he couldn't afford to keep such a daughter any longer. So, as she had grown into a beautiful young woman, he took her to the high king of Ireland to see if he would like to buy her as a slave.

He left Brigid at the palace door while he went in to see the king. The king himself came out to see Brigid and found that she had just given away her father's sword to a man who had come by, begging for food.

"But why give him my sword?" exploded her father. "It was valuable. It had jewels on the handle. What use was it to him?"

"But I had to give him something," she answered. "He was so thin and hungry."

"Hm!" said the king. "She's no good to me if she gives things away like this."

Brigid's father took her home again. Sometime after this, Brigid gained her father's permission to become a nun. This she did, along with some friends of her own age.

Once they were nuns, they visited the poor and sick, taking food to the hungry, nursing people who were ill, and teaching and helping children who had no parents. Because of this work, they became the first nuns to be known as the Sisters of Mercy.

Soon after Brigid became a nun, she found a place where she felt she would like to stay for the rest of her life. It was not far from a lake, and there was a great oak tree growing there. With the help of her friends, she built a hut, or cell, beneath the oak. Her friends built huts for themselves as well, and soon other women came to join them and to live as nuns.

As time went on, this collection of huts became a proper convent. Later, a town was built there too – known today as Kildare. Its name in Irish is *Kell-dura*, which means "the cell under the oak".

From this place, Brigid and her sister nuns would travel about the district, helping the poor. They also spent much time teaching people who visited them and making copies of holy books.

Benedict

SAINT'S DAY

11 JULY
(sometimes observed on 21 March)

Benedict was born in 480 in Nursia in what is now Italy. He went to Rome as a student, but he left to become a hermit when he was twenty. He then lived in a mountain cave near Subiaco, to the east of Rome. His holy way of living brought him many followers and he started a number of monasteries in the area. In the year 529, Benedict left Subiaco for Monte Cassino. His twin sister, Scholastica, became a nun and lived in a convent nearby. Benedict died in the year 550.

MONTE CASSINO HAS always been famous. It's a mountain (*monte* is Italian for mountain or mount) near the town of Cassino, which is southeast of Rome. First, the Romans built a temple there to their god Jupiter. Then Benedict came along and rebuilt it as a Christian monastery.

There is still a monastery on Monte Cassino, but it's not the same building. The one Benedict built in 529 was destroyed when the countryside around it was invaded fifty years later. Afterward, it was rebuilt, then destroyed three more times. On the first of these occasions, it was again wrecked by invaders. Then an earthquake did its worst. Finally, it was destroyed in 1944, during World War II. The area was occupied by Nazi soldiers at the time, and the damage was done by bombs. But every time it was destroyed, it was lovingly rebuilt.

Through all of this, the way of life of the monks who live there has changed very little. Just as the monks in the Eastern Church followed (and still follow) the Rule of Saint Basil, so the monks of Monte Cassino follow the Rule that Benedict planned for them.

Basil wrote his Rule in Greek. Benedict wrote his in Latin. He began it by saying he didn't want to make it too strict or his monks would get discouraged when they failed to keep it. But he didn't want to make it too easy either.

In his Prologue he refers to these words from the Psalms:

> *Come, my young friends, and listen to me,*
> *and I will teach you to honour the Lord.*
> *Would you like to enjoy life?*
> *Do you want long life and happiness?*
> *Then hold back from speaking evil*
> *and from telling lies.*
> *Turn away from evil and do good;*
> *strive for peace with all your heart.*

PSALM 34:11–14

His Rule said that his fellow monks (known as Benedictines) should meet in church several times a day to pray and to listen to Bible readings. But he said it was just as important that the monks should work. They should grow all their own food, prepare their own meals, mend the monastery when necessary, and copy books in beautiful handwriting. As he said, "To work is to pray." He also believed that "idleness is the enemy of the soul".

Unlike some monks and hermits of that time who slept little and who fasted often, Benedict said his monks should have eight hours' sleep every night and proper meals every day. He also believed that his monastery should help the people who lived in the district around it.

He also realized how difficult it was to get up for a church service in the middle of the night. "When the monks rise, let them gently encourage one another because the sleepy ones are likely to make excuses not to get up."

It is no wonder that this strict but kind man became so popular. His Rule is still followed by Benedictine communities all around the world. His sister, Scholastica, also inspired many people to take up a monastic way of living.

David

Saint's Day

1 March

David (or, in Welsh, Dewi) was the son of a Welsh prince and is thought to have been born in 520 near the present town of St Davids. The ruins of a small chapel dedicated to his mother, Non, can be seen near St Davids Cathedral. The story of his life was not written down until about 500 years after his death in 601. However, David was certainly a very holy man and is the only Welsh saint to be officially recognized by the Roman Catholic Church.

IT WAS ALWAYS the same meal – bread and vegetables and a little salt. That was all David allowed his monks to eat. Unlike Benedict, David believed monks needed to live a strict life. And he never allowed them to drink wine or beer – only water. That is how he got his nickname, David the Waterman.

It is said that, when he was a young man, he went from his homeland to the Isle of Wight in southern England to study the Bible and the teachings of Jesus with a wise old man named Paulinus. When Paulinus was getting old, he started to go blind. David touched his eyes, and once again Paulinus could see.

David was made a priest and returned to his homeland, Wales. He built no fewer than twelve monasteries. These included one at Glastonbury in

England and one at a place in the far west of Wales, which was then known as Menevia. That was where David himself settled, and Menevia is now named St Davids.

Life in David's monastery was not easy, and not just with regard to food and drink. Most of the day had to be spent in silence, and no sleep was allowed between Friday evening and Sunday morning. And David did not let his monks use any oxen or horses to plough the fields. "Each monk is his own ox. He must pull the plough himself."

He himself would often pray throughout the night, rather than going to bed. He also had a very strange habit. Sometimes he would stand up to his neck in icy water, just as a test to prove he could do this without complaining! Despite all this, he was much loved by everyone who heard him preach.

One day, there was a huge meeting in Wales at a place named Llanddewi Brefi. Thousands of people came to hear their bishops speak, but because the crowd was so big, it was impossible for everyone to hear what was being said. First one bishop tried and then another.

But old Paulinus was in the crowd. He remembered his pupil, David. "Let David speak," he said. "You'll be able to hear him."

At first, David didn't want to. He was only a

priest and not a bishop. But he prayed to God and then spoke clearly. Everyone, even those at the far edges of the crowd, could hear what he had to say. It is said that while he was talking, a white dove perched on his shoulder. People took this as a sign that God liked what he had to say.

A much stranger story says that before he started to speak, he put a handkerchief on the ground. When he stood on it, the ground under it rose up, and David was soon standing high enough to be seen as well as heard by everyone.

After this, David was made not only a bishop but archbishop (or head bishop) of Wales. He became highly regarded throughout South Wales, where fifty churches bear his name. For many years, his saint's day was celebrated as a religious festival. Later, it became a national festival among the Welsh, and Saint David's Day is now celebrated by Welsh people all over the world.

Columba of Iona and *Kentigern*

9 JUNE
Columba of Iona

13 JANUARY
Kentigern (Mungo)

Columba was born in Donegal, in Ireland, in 521.
He became a monk and later a priest, and he founded
many monasteries and churches in Ireland. In 563, he
moved to the island of Iona. It was said of him in later
years: "He had the face of an angel, he was of excellent
nature, polished in speech, holy in deed… and loving
unto all." By then, he was known as Columba the
Dove. Kentigern was born in Scotland in 518 and
became a monk. Over the years, he was given the
nickname "Mungo", meaning "darling". Kentigern
died in 603.

Columba and Kentigern were both Celtic saints.
The word "Celtic" is used to describe people
who have lived in the western parts of the British
Isles, such as Ireland and Scotland, over the last
thousand years.

COLUMBA OF IONA

NOT MANY SAINTS have been responsible for the
deaths of three thousand men. You certainly
wouldn't suspect a saint nicknamed "the Dove".

The truth is that although Columba (who was a
Celt and an Irishman) may have been a very gentle
and loving man in his middle and old age, he had
a temper when he was young. The trouble began
with a book.

In those days, before printing was invented, if you wanted a book, you had to make a copy of it by hand. The young monk Columba loved books and made hundreds of copies of holy books in his own beautiful handwriting.

One time, he borrowed a book without permission and secretly made a copy of it for himself. Its owner, a man named Finnian, had got the book while visiting Rome. He claimed that because he owned the original, the copy must belong to him as well.

This led to a court case to see who had the "copy right". The high king of Ireland decided the case against Columba, saying, "To every cow, her calf. To every book, its copy. Therefore the copy you made, Columba, must be restored to Finnian."

Columba was angry. It seems that he and his followers started a war against the high king, and it was during this war that three thousand men were killed. When he realized what had happened as a result of losing his temper, Columba was deeply sorry. He decided that he must leave Ireland for ever and bring to Jesus as many souls as had lost their lives in the battle.

He and twelve close friends set sail in tiny boats, eventually landing on a small island off the western coast of Scotland. We now know the island as Iona.

It's less than three miles long and two miles wide, and there they buried their boats and built a simple monastery. The main building was a tiny wooden church, surrounded by the small huts in which they lived.

They spent their time farming the stony soil, fishing, raising animals – and making beautiful copies of holy books. All the work stopped at regular times for services in the little church.

Once this little group of monks was settled on Iona, Columba began journeying around the mainland of Scotland, teaching the message of Jesus. His first aim was to persuade the Scottish kings and chiefs. He knew that if one of them became Christian, then the people would follow. Columba did succeed in persuading the king of Inverness to become a Christian, and from then on, his work was easier.

Columba died in his little church on Iona in 597, exactly one week after Augustine baptized the king of Kent and established Christianity in southern England. By this time, Columba had led many more than three thousand people to the Christian way of life.

Delightful I think it to be
in the bosom of an isle

on the crest of a rock,
that I may see often
the calm of the sea.

That I may see its heavy waves
over the glittering ocean
as they chant a melody
to their Father
on their eternal course.

That I may bless the Lord
who has power over all,
heaven with its crystal orders of angels,
earth, ebb, flood-tide.

SAINT COLUMBA AT IONA

KENTIGERN

KENTIGERN WAS ALSO a Celt. He was a Scottish monk who lived in what was once very peaceful countryside where Glasgow now stands. He journeyed around, preaching the Christian faith, and may have met Saint Columba and also visited Saint David in Wales. A famous story told about him explains why there is a fish and a ring on the crest of the city of Glasgow.

The king of Strathclyde had given his queen a very precious ring. One day, he saw it – not on

135

her finger, but on the finger of one of his knights who happened to be asleep. Not surprisingly, the king was both angry and jealous. The king gently slipped the ring from the knight's finger and flung it into the River Clyde. He then asked his queen to show him the ring.

Not knowing what to do, she asked Kentigern for his help. He told one of his monks to go fishing that night and bring back the first fish that he caught.

The next day, the monk brought Kentigern the fish. It was a salmon. When it was cut open, there inside was the ring that the fish had swallowed. The queen was able to take the ring and show it to her surprised husband.

Gregory, Augustine of Canterbury, and Ethelbert

SAINTS' DAYS

3 SEPTEMBER
Gregory

26 OR 27 MAY
Augustine of Canterbury

24 FEBRUARY
Ethelbert

*Pope Gregory was keen to send missionaries
throughout western Europe to spread the Christian
gospel. One of these was Augustine, whom he sent
to England. Gregory loved music and encouraged
a special kind of chanting in church services, now
known as Gregorian chant or "plainsong". He also
reorganized the calendar and wrote many books.
Even in his lifetime, he was famous for his huge
bald head. Both Gregory and Augustine died in 604.
King Ethelbert gave much help to Augustine and his
followers, and arranged for the building of the first
Saint Paul's Cathedral in London. He died in 616.*

G REGORY WALKED THROUGH Rome's marketplace.
He turned a corner and found himself facing
a slave master selling some young boy slaves. Most
slaves in Rome were imported from North Africa
or the East, but these lads were not dark-skinned.
Instead, they had blond hair and fair skin.

"Who are they, and where are they from?" asked
Gregory.

"They're Angles, from Deira."

"Then they must be rescued from *Dei ira*,"
answered Gregory, who could never resist making
a pun. For, although Deira was the name of part of
the island where the Angles lived, the Latin words
Dei ira also mean "the anger of God".

And that is how Pope Gregory decided he must send someone to spread the Christian message to that part of the world, which we now know as England. The man he chose was a monk named Augustine, who set off from Rome with forty companions in the year 596. The Romans no longer ruled Europe. Much of the North was overrun with brigands, robbers, and barbarians.

On his journey through France, Augustine became fearful and went back to Rome. But Gregory wasn't going to let him give up so easily. He ordered Augustine to complete his journey.

Augustine and his monks landed in Kent, in south-east England, in 597, again afraid. What might the pagan king of Kent do to them? They were in for a surprise.

King Ethelbert of Kent rode out to make them welcome. He listened to what they had to say and then gave them permission to enter his capital city, Canterbury, and to talk to people about Jesus. He also gave them somewhere to live, free of charge.

There was yet another surprise awaiting Augustine. The king's wife, Queen Bertha, was already a Christian. She was originally French and had become a Christian before marrying Ethelbert. He had allowed her to have a small Christian church in Canterbury, and that became Augustine's first base for his mission to the Angles.

Many of the Kentish people became Christian, including King Ethelbert himself, who was baptized at the festival of Pentecost in 597. Augustine followed the advice of Gregory not to destroy any pagan temples he found. Instead, he blessed them for the use of Christians and put altars in them.

Augustine was made bishop of the English and archbishop of Canterbury, and King Ethelbert gave Augustine land on which, in time, the great Canterbury Cathedral was built.

Some say Augustine was rather bossy. Perhaps that is why he did not get on with the Christians in the west of the British Isles when he went to meet them at a place that later became known as Saint Augustine's Oak. Nor did he convert the northern part of the land of the Angles, named Deira, as Pope Gregory had intended. However, Augustine did establish Christianity as the main religion in southern England.

Hundreds of years later, Henry VIII declared himself head of the church in England, and the archbishop of Canterbury became its spiritual leader. The Anglican Church is now represented in many countries around the world, but Canterbury Cathedral remains its central focus.

Aidan,
Oswald,
and
Hilda of Whitby

SAINTS' DAYS

31 AUGUST
Aidan

5, 8, OR 9 AUGUST
Oswald

17 NOVEMBER
Hilda of Whitby

King Oswald of Northumbria was born in 604. He did
much to promote Christianity, with the help of a monk
named Aidan, who established a community on the
island of Lindisfarne. The Lindisfarne Gospels, copied
and beautifully decorated by the monks, survive and
are kept at the British Museum in London. Hilda was
born in 614, the great-niece of a king, and became the
abbess of Whitby in 657. Under her guidance, the abbey
developed as an important place of study and learning.

AIDAN AND OSWALD

O SWALD STOOD ON the battlements of his fine
castle, looking out over the long white sands
of Bamburgh beach. His kingdom of Northumbria
was at peace now, after he'd won that last battle.
Everything was fine. He just had one slight worry –
a promise he'd made and not yet kept.

The morning before that last battle, he'd made
a Christian cross out of wood, called all his soldiers
together, and made them kneel before it. Oswald
had then prayed aloud and promised God that if
he could drive the enemy away and bring peace to
Northumbria, he would do all he could to teach
his people about Jesus and the Christian religion –
something they knew nothing about.

As it turned out, the enemy was easily defeated.
Oswald returned to Bamburgh, where he was now

wondering how to keep his promise. He himself had heard about Christianity when he was a boy and his father had sent him north to an island named Iona. He'd been taught by the Christian monks there. And as he remembered his time at Iona, the answer became obvious. He'd send a messenger for a monk to come to Northumbria to teach his people.

The monk who came from Iona was named Aidan. Oswald wanted him to live comfortably in Bamburgh Castle, but Aidan politely said no.

"I'd like to live on an island like Iona, a place apart where I can be quiet and pray and read, but not so far away that I can't reach the mainland and the people of your land."

"I have the perfect place," replied Oswald. "We know it as Lindisfarne. You can see it from here. Six miles by boat, more if you insist on walking."

"You can walk to this island?" asked Aidan.

The king laughed. "It's only an island at high tide. When the tide goes out, you can walk across the sand to reach it."

Aidan settled on what came to be known as Holy Island. Other monks came and they built a church and places to sleep and eat. They built a guest house and a hospital – and they kept bees. From the bees' wax they made candles, and from their honey, they made a drink known as mead.

Aidan also spent time going around Northumbria teaching the people about Jesus, and King Oswald often went with him. In time, Aidan became bishop of Northumbria.

All was well until the fierce army of King Penda, a cruel and pagan king, came north from the land of Mercia, attacking towns and villages and stealing from the people. Oswald locked himself inside his castle.

Outside, close to the south gate, Penda's men built a huge bonfire. They stole thatch and wood from all the houses round about and set fire to it. Soon the castle itself would be on fire, and Oswald would be captured or burned to death.

Across the bay on Lindisfarne, Aidan and another monk whose name was James watched. Then they felt a south wind that made the fire burn all the more fiercely. Aidan prayed hard, and the wind changed direction, blowing the fire back toward Penda's men. Soon they were fleeing, and Bamburgh Castle and King Oswald were saved.

HILDA OF WHITBY

AIDAN NEEDED SOMEONE to do a special job – to be in charge of a "double monastery". Half of this monastery was for monks. The other half was for nuns. It was at Hartlepool in north-east

England, and the monk who'd been running it was not very efficient.

"Hilda is the obvious person to take it on," said Aidan.

Hilda was a nun who was a great organizer. When she was around, people knew things wouldn't go wrong. She was also fair, kind, and patient. As Saint Bede later wrote, "No wonder everyone thought of her as 'mother'."

"But she's a woman," said one of Aidan's Lindisfarne monks, who was set in his ways.

"It should be the best person for the job," replied Aidan. "And that's Hilda."

Seven years later, the problems at Hartlepool Abbey had been sorted out, and it was time for Hilda to move on. She went to Whitby, a little further south on the Yorkshire coast, to start another double monastery for monks and nuns there.

Hilda was famous for her good advice. She told someone who had a plague of snakes how to get rid of them. She advised some villagers on what to do when their crops were being eaten by a flock of wild geese. Even kings and princes came to ask for help when they had problems.

In the year 664, a great conference, or synod, of church leaders was to be held.

"Whitby is the obvious place to have it,"

everyone said. "Hilda will see everything goes all right."

The churches in Britain were divided. On the one side were the churches in the west of England, in Wales and Ireland and Scotland, sometimes known as the Celtic churches. They had first heard about Christianity from people like Patrick, David, and Columba.

On the other side were the churches in southern England who had first heard about Christianity from Augustine of Canterbury.

Various things divided them. They argued about when Easter Sunday should be each year. The Celtic monks thought the Benedictine monks in southern England lived in too much comfort. The Synod of Whitby was being held to sort everything out.

After much argument, they agreed to follow the ways of Canterbury, mainly because they were also the ways of Christians all over Europe, Africa, and Asia. Hilda had been on the side of the Celtic Christians, but she made sure that all the decisions of the synod were carried out.

Cuthbert

Saint's Day

20 MARCH (OR 4 SEPTEMBER)

Cuthbert was born in around 634 and became a monk in 651, the year Aidan died. After a time living as a hermit on the island of Inner Farne, Cuthbert became a bishop – first of Hexham and then of Lindisfarne. It is said that he loved birds and animals, and that they loved him. He died on Inner Farne in 687 and was buried on Lindisfarne. When the Vikings came raiding, his body was moved. It now rests in Durham Cathedral.

CUTHBERT NEVER FORGOT the moment. It happened when he was about nine. He was playing with some friends when one of the boys came up to him and said, "Bishop Cuthbert, why do you play with children when God has marked you out to teach grown-ups?"

This stayed in the back of his mind until he was sixteen. By then, he was earning his living as a shepherd, guarding sheep on the hills of Northumbria in north-east England. One night, as he was keeping watch, a pathway of light suddenly appeared in the sky. A number of angels seemed to be passing upward on it. Somehow Cuthbert knew that they were carrying up to heaven the soul of someone who had just died.

He woke the other shepherds to tell them what he'd seen.

"Rubbish," they laughed.

But he wasn't put off. He set off down the hill to a cluster of huts not far away. Here lived a group of monks who had come from their monastery on Lindisfarne, also known as Holy Island.

They didn't laugh at his story. While they were wondering what it might mean, a messenger arrived from Lindisfarne. The previous night, just at the time when Cuthbert had seen the light in the sky, Brother Aidan had died.

It all seemed to make sense to Cuthbert. Surely God was calling him to be a monk?

Cuthbert did indeed become a monk. He spent much of his time journeying around Northumbria, meeting people Aidan had met, and reminding them of the teachings of Jesus. Having grown up in that area, Cuthbert had the advantage of speaking the local language.

Some years later, Saint Bede described Cuthbert's journeys: "He made a point of searching out those steep, rugged places in the hills that other preachers dreaded to visit because of their poverty and squalor."

Once Cuthbert was on a journey with a young lad and they'd run out of food.

"We're going to die of hunger," said the boy.

"Those who serve God will never be hungry.

See, up there." Cuthbert pointed to a bird of prey in the sky. At that moment, the bird swooped down, snatched a fish from a nearby river, and landed on the riverbank to eat it. "Run and get what God has sent."

The boy did so and came back with the fish.

"Cut it in two and put half back for the bird. We'll cook the other half."

One time, as a way of trying to make himself more humble, he walked into the icy North Sea up to his armpits and stood there, praying. A number of seals swam up and nuzzled up to him as though to keep him warm.

Another time, he saw a flock of birds eating the monastery's crop of barley. When he spoke to them, they flew away.

After some years, Cuthbert became a hermit on the small island of Inner Farne, not far from Lindisfarne and Bamburgh. There he lived on a stone bed, meeting occasional visitors and surrounded by his special friends – the seals and sea birds. He was particularly fond of the eider ducks, which are even now sometimes called Cuthbert's ducks.

A tiny chapel still stands on Inner Farne, on the island where Cuthbert lived and died.

Bede

SAINT'S DAY

25 MAY

Bede was born in 673. He wrote many historical and scientific books, including the first history of the English church, Ecclesiastical History of the English People. *It was written in Latin but translated into Anglo-Saxon by order of King Alfred. Bede was especially clever at working out what had actually happened in the past and what was only legend or gossip. It is thanks to Bede that we know so much about such saints as Aidan, Cuthbert, and Hilda. He died in 735.*

DEATH IS NEVER a happy event. But it's hard to imagine a happier, more peaceful death than that of Bede. He was both a monk and a priest and he'd spent almost all his life in a Benedictine monastery at a place called Jarrow in north-east England. Now he was an old man, tired and weak.

He had been taken seriously ill a fortnight before Easter Sunday, but continued his work of translating John's Gospel from Greek into Anglo-Saxon, or Early English, the language then spoken in much of England. In those days, all books were handwritten, using quill pens and ink. When he was younger, Bede used to write his own books. Now he dictated what he wanted to say to an assistant, a young monk named Wilbert.

On the Tuesday before Ascension Day (the day

that recalls how Jesus ended his work on earth),
Bede knew he was close to death. All that night, he
lay awake, but at dawn, he insisted that the work
should carry on. Lying on his narrow bed, Bede
dictated slowly with Wilbert writing down what he
said until it was three o'clock in the afternoon.

Bede then said, "There are some things of value
in my chest, such as peppercorns, napkins, and
incense. Run quickly and get them and bring the
other priests of the monastery to me."

After distributing his possessions, he asked the
priests to pray for him. He said, "You shall see my
face no more in this life. My soul longs to see Christ
my king in heaven in all his beauty."

When evening came, Wilbert noticed that one
sentence of the passage they were translating was
unfinished.

"Write it," said Bede.

Wilbert wrote down the words Bede dictated.
"Master, now it's finished," he said.

Bede lay down on the floor of the little room.
"You have spoken truthfully. It is well finished."
They had reached chapter six of John's Gospel.

Then Bede asked Wilbert to raise his head, and
he sang, "Glory be to the Father, and to the Son,
and to the Holy Spirit." As he chanted the last
word, he breathed his last breath and died.

But what of Bede's life? At the age of seven, he'd been sent away to a monastery to be educated. By the time he was ten, he was living in the monastery at Jarrow. He spent the rest of his life there, never going further north than Lindisfarne, never going further south than York. He wrote, "I have devoted my energies to the study of the Bible... Study, teaching, and writing have always been my delight."

Bede wrote a very important history book. It tells the story of the English church from the time of the Romans up to his own lifetime. Because of this, Bede is often known as the father of English history.

Soon after his death in 735, he was given the title "the Venerable Bede". The title "Venerable" means "worthy" and is given to people who are likely to be made saints in the future. Amazingly, the church did not officially make this holy man a saint until 1899.

Boniface

SAINT'S DAY

5 JUNE

Boniface was born in 680 at Crediton in south-west
England and entered a monastery at the age of five!
As a priest, he became one of the great missionaries of
the church, bringing the Christian gospel to much of
Germany, including Bavaria and Hesse, as well as to
parts of France and the Low Countries. He founded
many monasteries, nunneries, and schools, and was
made archbishop of Mainz. In 754, he was murdered,
along with fifty-two companions, by a band of pagan
Frieslanders. Many of his letters survive. He also wrote
the first Latin textbook to be used in English schools.

I T WAS A huge tree. A great sturdy oak, growing
near the town of Geismar in what was later to
be known as East Germany. It stood near the top
of Mount Gudenberg and it was sacred to the great
Norse god of thunder, Thor.

That, at least, was what the local people said. So,
naturally enough, when this Englishman turned
up and said he was going to cut the tree down,
they were horrified. What would Thor do to such
a man? Strike him dead with lightning seemed
the most likely answer. They were also not a little
terrified for themselves. Surely Thor would punish
them for allowing anyone to damage, never mind
destroy, his precious oak tree?

In the end, a huge crowd decided it was worth

that risk. They'd climb Mount Gudenberg and watch the Englishman get struck by lightning.

The Englishman's name was Boniface, and he was both a monk and a priest. He'd come to what was then a pagan land to teach its people the Christian message of love and hope, and he'd spent two years learning their language in order to be able to do this.

Now he wanted to prove that the old Norse gods such as Thor had no power over a Christian believer. More than that, he wanted to prove that the Norse gods weren't even real.

So he climbed the hill to the so-called "Thor's Oak" with a few fellow monks and a large axe. The local people followed. They felt safe – and certain that Thor would know who was damaging his oak. He would surely strike Boniface dead for this terrible insult to him and his tree.

Boniface gripped the axe and took a mighty swing. The blade sank into the trunk of the tree. Boniface wrenched it free and took another swipe. Again the blade sank into the wood.

By now, there was a rustling in its upper branches. A wind was getting up. The crowd all had the same thought: Thor's getting angry.

Boniface and his monks dealt a few more blows to the tree. Now its upper branches were shaking violently. Then, with a mighty creak and a groan, the tree shuddered and began to fall. As its upper branches toppled to the ground, they broke and splintered.

The locals were positive that Thor had shown his power. Boniface must be dead under the weight of the trunk. But he stepped smiling out of the pile of broken branches and shook some twigs out of his monk's habit.

"So what have you to say now?" he asked. "Where was Thor? I told you he wasn't real."

The people had to admit that Thor appeared to have no power over a Christian. Some immediately decided to become Christians. Over the days and weeks that followed, more and more followed their example. Soon much of the area was Christian.

As for the tree, Boniface chopped and sawed it up and used the wood to build a small wooden church on that very spot, naming the church Saint Peter's.

Margaret of Scotland

Saint's Day

16 NOVEMBER
(or, in some countries, 10 June)

Margaret was born in Hungary, probably in 1045, and was linked to two royal families. Her father was the son of an English king, Edmund Ironside; her mother was related to King Stephen of Hungary. Margaret arrived in England in 1057 and left for Scotland in 1067. She did much to help link the Scottish church (which still clung to its old Celtic ways, despite the Synod of Whitby) with the wider church. She was the first to bring Benedictine monks to Scotland, and she re-established Iona as a holy place. She died in 1093 and is one of the few married women saints.

I N THE YEAR 1066, William the Conqueror invaded England, won the Battle of Hastings, and became king. It became clear that the English court was no longer a safe place for the young Princess Margaret.

She was just twenty-two. With her mother, she'd been brought to England ten years earlier and had grown up in the court of the kindly King Edward, known as Edward the Confessor because of his holiness. But he had died, his son had been killed, and the new King William didn't want anyone around who'd been connected with that family.

So before he could harm the princess, her mother decided they must escape. But where should they go? France was out of the question:

William ruled there as well. The answer seemed to be Scotland.

They went by sea. It wasn't good weather, but at last, they arrived safely. King Malcolm of Scotland welcomed them. After all, he knew what it was like to be a royal refugee. Some years earlier, he'd had to flee for his life when his own father, King Duncan, had been murdered by a man named Macbeth.

But he not only welcomed the beautiful princess, he fell in love with her, and they were married three years later.

Now it has to be said they were an odd couple. She was quiet, holy, prayerful, kind, and generous. He was different. To be blunt, he was noisy, rough, rude, and fond of war. And his palace where they lived at Dunfermline was grim, bleak, and cold.

Margaret set about changing her husband, his palace, and the country. She helped him control his temper. She brought bright hangings and tapestries to the castle – and she brought books. In particular, she had a beautiful illustrated copy of the Gospels. But she never managed to teach Malcolm to read. She did however persuade him that books were important, and he would kiss the Bible to show he respected it.

Gradually, she made the court more beautiful and refined. The courtiers began to join her at her prayers. Every day, she opened the palace doors to the sick and the poor and personally gave food to those in need. Twenty-four people lived entirely at her expense, and when she journeyed around Scotland, she carried money to give to those who were hungry. If she ran out of money, she used Malcolm's. He learned not to notice when this happened.

But all was not well between Scotland and England. The two countries began fighting each other, and during this war, Malcolm was killed. So too was their eldest son.

At the same time, Margaret had become ill. When a younger son returned from the battle, she asked him how they were. So as not to worry her, he said they were well.

She replied, "I know how it is." Four days later, she prayed to God, "Let me be free." Then she died.

Bernard of Clairvaux

SAINT'S DAY

20 AUGUST

Bernard was born in 1090 and grew up in a castle near Dijon in France. He became a monk in 1113 and went to Clairvaux in 1115. In 1146, he toured Europe, persuading men to fight the Turks in Palestine in the Second Crusade. But too many joined the vast army and there was not enough food for them all. Thousands died of hunger and illness before reaching the Holy Land. Bernard was, however, a great teacher and healer. He died in 1153.

IT WAS CHRISTMAS. Bernard was eight, and he was dreaming that he was in Bethlehem and that Mary was letting him kiss the baby Jesus. From then on, he became very religious.

Bernard's father was a wealthy nobleman, and Bernard's two elder brothers, Guido and Gérard, grew up to become soldiers. Not so Bernard. He wasn't strong, but he was intelligent. He was sent away to school and became very learned. When he was twenty-two, he decided to become a monk.

Bernard went to his Uncle Gaudry (himself a nobleman and a soldier) and asked what he thought about his plan.

"Great idea," said Gaudry, to Bernard's surprise.

Bernard's cousins didn't agree. "You're rich. Why give it all up?"

"I still think it's a good idea," said Gaudry.

"And I might follow his example."

To the family's dismay, the two of them set off to join a monastery at a place named Cîteaux. But first, Bernard had a chat with his younger brother, Bartholomew. He too decided to join them.

Encouraged, Bernard then visited the army camp to see his elder brother Guido and yet another brother, Andrew. Andrew refused to become a monk. At first, Guido said no too, for he was married.

"Oh don't worry about that," said Bernard. "Your wife'll say it's all right."

And eventually she did let Guido go. That left Gérard. He was hoping to get a promotion, and would not leave the army.

Sadly, a few days later, he was captured.

Meanwhile, it was time for Bernard to go to Cîteaux. He went to say goodbye to a school friend named Hugh of Macon. A day later, Hugh decided to join Bernard. So did another friend named Geoffrey. It was no wonder that by now wives and mothers were saying, "Look out, it's Bernard. Hide your husbands, hide your sons. Otherwise he'll take them off to be monks."

In the end, thirty-two of them went to Cîteaux, including Gérard, who had managed to escape from prison.

Cîteaux was a Cistercian monastery and much

165

stricter than a Benedictine one. That was why Bernard chose it. "My weak character needs strong medicine," he explained.

Cistercian monks were known as "white friars" because they wore plain, undyed habits. Benedictines, who dyed theirs black, were known as "black friars".

At first, the abbey of Cîteaux had little food for Bernard and its new monks. Bernard prayed about it. Shortly afterward, a woman gave them money as way of saying thank you to God for her husband's recovery from an illness.

Two years after arriving at Cîteaux, Bernard was asked to build a new monastery. The place he chose was in the part of France known as Champagne. Because of the monastery, it became known as "the valley of light" or, in French, Clairvaux.

Bernard became famous throughout Europe. He wasn't afraid to tell kings when he thought they were doing wrong. Once there was an argument about which of two men should be pope, and he persuaded everyone who should be chosen. He was, after all, very good at persuading people to do what he wanted, and was nicknamed "Doctor Mellifluous" or "the honey-sweet teacher".

Thomas Becket

SAINT'S DAY

29 DECEMBER

Thomas was born in London in 1118. His parents
were well off and he was given a good education.
He studied law, and King Henry II made him royal
chancellor and then archbishop of Canterbury. But
Thomas's refusal to do as Henry wished made the
king furious, and in 1170, Thomas was brutally
murdered in Canterbury Cathedral. After he was
declared a saint, the cathedral became a popular place
of pilgrimage.

L IKE SO MANY things, it began with a quarrel.
Several quarrels, in fact – all between
King Henry II of England and Thomas Becket,
archbishop of Canterbury.

Thomas Becket was the son of a rich merchant.
He'd done very well for himself, getting better
and better jobs. Then the king made him royal
chancellor, responsible for seeing that everything
the king ordered was carried out. So Thomas was
powerful. He lived in his own luxurious palace and
enjoyed good food, fine clothes, and hunting.

Meanwhile, Henry had a problem. He was
having trouble getting the leaders of the church,
the bishops, to do what he wanted. They didn't like
being bossed around and felt that not even the king
should tell the church what to do.

Then Henry had an idea. If he made his friend

Thomas archbishop of Canterbury, he would be in charge of all the bishops, and they would have to do what Thomas said. And of course, as Thomas was Henry's friend, that would mean the king would get his own way.

Thomas was made archbishop. He gave up his luxurious way of life and began to live very simply. What mattered most to him now was the church. He took its part against the king. So it was little wonder that they soon argued so seriously that Thomas had to leave England for his own safety. In 1164, he went to live in Rome.

Six years later, when Thomas and Henry were both in France, they met and made up their quarrel. Thomas returned to Canterbury. The people treated him as a hero and cheered as he made his way into the city. Again Thomas became the champion of the church, and soon the king's temper flared up again.

One December day, while he was still in France, Henry shouted, "Who will free me from this turbulent priest?"

Four of the king's knights heard and decided the king could mean only one thing. They looked at each other and nodded.

And so, those knights, Sir William de Tracy, Reginald FitzUrse, Richard le Breton, and Hugh de

Morville, rode north as fast as they could and took a ship across the Channel. Some people say that Henry sent messengers after them to stop them. If he did, they failed to catch up with the four knights.

Four days after Christmas, the knights arrived in Canterbury and met Thomas. An argument took place. Thomas went into the cathedral to pray at one of the altars. The priests of the cathedral wanted to bar and lock the doors. Thomas said no, the church of God should not be locked. Then, just as it was getting dark, the knights made their way in and there, in a holy part of the cathedral, with their great heavy swords, they struck down Thomas and killed him.

Christians all over Europe were horrified when they heard what had happened and soon people started to call him Saint Thomas Becket. It wasn't long before people started making journeys to Canterbury to pray where Saint Thomas was buried.

In the end, King Henry realized how much he was to blame. He too visited Canterbury, walking barefoot to show how sorry he was and kneeling to pray at the grave of the man who had been his best friend.

Francis of Assisi

SAINT'S DAY

4 OCTOBER

Francis was born in around 1181, and originally named John. He was nicknamed Francis (Francesco in Italian, meaning "little Frenchman") because his father often went to France on business. In 1210, the pope allowed Francis to set up a new order of monks, or friars, known as Franciscans. Francis was famous for his love of animals and birds, and is the patron saint of ecologists. He is also remembered for his reconstruction of the story of Jesus' birth and the visit of the shepherds – the first Nativity play. He died in 1226.

PETER BERNARDONE WAS furious. It was all to do with his boy, Francis.

Peter Bernardone was a rich merchant who lived in the Italian town of Assisi and bought and sold silk, linen, and other expensive cloths. He wanted his son to enjoy the same sort of life as the other wealthy young noblemen of the town.

At first, Francis had liked going to parties and spending money. But then he was ill for a while. As he got better, he started to spend more time on his own, praying. Whenever he could, he gave his money and food to poor people. He no longer wore his fine, expensive clothes.

One day, he was praying in a church named Saint Damian's, just outside Assisi. The church was old and almost in ruins. As Francis prayed in front of a large crucifix (a cross with a statue of Jesus on it), the statue seemed to speak: "Francis, repair my church."

At that time, his father was away on business. So Francis went back home, sold some of his father's goods, and took the money to the priest at Saint Damian's to pay for the repairs.

When Peter Bernardone returned and found out what had happened, he almost exploded with anger. He grabbed his son and led him off to see the bishop.

The bishop listened to the whole story. Turning to Francis, he said gently, "Francis, the church cannot take what does not belong to it. You must give back to your father what is his."

So Francis took the money and gave it back to his father. Then he tore off all his clothes and threw them at him. "Now I owe you nothing, Father! I've got nothing of yours," he said. "You're no longer my father, and I've no father but my Father in heaven."

Peter Bernardone stormed out. Someone put an old workman's tunic around Francis. His new life had begun.

From that day, Francis lived very simply, owning nothing, eating only the food he could beg, and wearing a rough brown cloak, or tunic. Other young men gave up everything and joined him. They became known as Franciscans. They moved from place to place, helping the poor, comforting those who were ill or dying, and greeting everyone with the words, "The peace of God be with you."

Although their life was a little like that of monks, they were called "friars", or brothers. Francis wrote down a "Rule" for their way of life. The friars were to promise to live in poverty and to have no possessions; they could not marry nor have any kind of love life, and they were to be obedient at all times. This Rule was later approved by the pope. Present-day followers of Saint Francis still live by the same Rule.

Despite this strict Rule, Franciscans have always been cheerful. Francis thought it was wrong to be gloomy and encouraged his followers to smile and laugh whenever possible.

He also became famous for his kindness to animals and birds. One day, Francis standing on a little hill, teaching a group of people about God.

"What God wants us to do is – " said Francis.

"We can't hear you!" interrupted the people.

It was true. They couldn't. A large number of swallows were building nests nearby and chirping very loudly.

"My dear sister swallows," said Francis, "listen to the word of God and be quiet till I've finished."

To everyone's amazement, the swallows all became silent.

"Thank you," said Francis. "As I was saying, what God wants us to do is to love each other. Be kind to each other. We are all brothers and sisters – even the animals and birds. That is why I call the swallows 'sisters'."

The swallows kept silent until he had finished teaching. Then, once again, they began to sing.

Just before Christmas, in the year 1223, Francis decided to show the people who lived around a place named Grecchio exactly what it had been like for Jesus to be born in a stable.

"Friar John," he said to one of his older followers. "I want to talk to you about Christmas."

"You are going to spend it with us, aren't you? Here at Grecchio?" asked the old man, afraid that Francis might be leaving them.

"Yes, I shall spend Christmas here," said Francis. "But I want all the people from the valley to understand what it was like. John, I want you to arrange something for me."

Together they made a plan. Francis asked all

the people from the villages around to come to Grecchio on Christmas Eve, bringing a lighted torch or candle.

At the entrance to a cave, Friar John had placed a manger – the kind of wooden trough that holds hay for animals to eat. Beside it were a man and a woman looking into the manger where a little bundle of clothes represented a baby. There were other men there dressed up as shepherds, together with a real ox and an ass.

When the people saw this, they said, "But that's just how it must have been in Bethlehem when Jesus was born."

Francis was pleased. "Yes. That's how it was. He was born in a simple stable among brother and sister animals. Let's sing and give thanks to God for sending Jesus to us that very first Christmas."

And that is what Christians have done at Christmas ever since.

May we love our neighbours as ourselves;
drawing them all to your love in so far as we can,
sharing their good fortune as if it were our own,
helping them to bear their trials
and doing them no wrong.

WORDS OF SAINT FRANCIS

Clare and
Antony of Padua

SAINTS' DAYS

11 AUGUST
Clare

13 JUNE
Antony of Padua

*The work of Francis of Assisi was continued by two of
his close friends, Clare and Antony. Clare was born in
1194 and died in 1253. She founded the order of nuns
known as the "Poor Clares". Antony was a priest who
became a greatly respected teacher and preacher. He
was made a saint just one year after his death in 1231,
a sign that he was much loved by Christians of his day.*

CLARE

T HEY SEARCHED THE whole house. Clare, the
beautiful eighteen-year-old daughter of the
wealthy Count Offreduccio, could not be found.
It was the evening of Palm Sunday in 1212. That
morning, she had gone with all her family to
church in Assisi. Francis had been the preacher.

Clare and Francis had first met five years earlier
in the ruins of Saint Damian's Church. He'd
just given up all his wealth to live a life of simple
poverty. She'd met him regularly after that, and she
too had decided she wanted to serve Jesus through
poverty. Only one person knew of Clare's plan – her
younger sister, Agnes. Yet Clare had not told even
Agnes exactly when she would leave.

Clare had crept out of the house. She had made
her way out of the town and to a secret meeting
place, where she was met by Francis and some of
his new friars. There she exchanged her fine gown

for a simple habit tied with rope. Francis cut off her long, golden hair, and she covered her head with a veil. The Franciscans took Clare to a nearby Benedictine convent.

When her father discovered where she was, he tried to drag her away, but she clung to the altar of its church. On seeing her short hair, he gave up. Soon Agnes joined her.

After Francis had repaired Saint Damian's Church, Clare lived there with her followers. They never ate meat, they did without shoes and socks, and they had no personal property. In 1252, while in her convent, Clare "saw" in her mind a church service that was taking place at Assisi. Because of this, she was named patron saint of television in 1958.

The order of nuns that Clare established, a sister order to the Franciscans, are even now known as the Poor Clares.

ANTONY OF PADUA

ANTONY OF PADUA was born in Lisbon, in Portugal, in 1195. He was short and chubby, but had a voice that seemed to carry for miles. He lived quietly as a priest until he decided to visit Morocco in North Africa to spread the gospel there.

Soon after arriving, he became ill and had to

return to Portugal. But his ship was caught in a violent storm and blown toward Sicily. Later, Antony went to Italy and lived as a hermit.

One day, a number of Franciscan friars arrived for a service. No one had been chosen to preach, so the friars asked Antony to give the talk. He spoke so wisely that Francis appointed Antony to become a teacher to the Franciscan friars. He rapidly became a very famous and respected preacher, and is remembered for having preached a sermon to the fish of the sea (when some people wouldn't listen to him).

One day, a young monk borrowed Antony's prayer book without permission but returned it quickly because he thought he had seen a devil and he felt guilty. For this reason, Saint Antony is associated with things that have been lost, and some Christians pray to him to help them find lost objects.

Thomas Aquinas

Saint's Day

28 JANUARY

Thomas was born in 1225 and was educated by Benedictine monks before he joined the newly formed Dominicans. After finishing his studies, he taught in the universities of Paris, Orvieto, and Naples. He was a patient, good-natured man and was genuinely humble, despite his intelligence. Among the ideas he wrote about (which are part of the teaching of the Roman Catholic Church) was his belief that contraception and abortion are wrong. He died in the year 1274.

I T'S RIDICULOUS. You can't possibly do that. No son of mine should be seen begging!" Count Landulf of Aquino was furious. In front of him stood his nineteen-year-old son, Thomas.

"Father, I am going to join the Dominicans."

"You are going to join the Benedictines. I say so."

There was no doubt that Thomas (named Aquinas, after his father's hometown, Aquino) was going to be a monk. The argument was about which order of monks he should join. Count Landulf was a bit of a snob, as well as a very rich banker. He wanted his son to live in a respectable Benedictine monastery. The Dominicans didn't live in monasteries but went around teaching, helping those they met, and living on what people gave them.

"To think," spluttered Count Landulf, "to think that a son of mine should live like a common beggar."

Thomas had already tried to join the Dominicans in nearby Naples. As soon as his mother had heard about this, she'd hurried off to Naples to make him change his mind. By then, Thomas had gone to Rome. She'd followed after him, but by the time she got there, he'd moved on to Bologna. Eventually, his two elder brothers (who were soldiers) had managed to find him and bring him back to Aquino.

Since Thomas refused to change his mind, his father now decided to lock him up in a room in the castle. "He'll soon do what I say," he said.

Thomas didn't. Not even when his brothers played a trick on him, hoping to prove he wasn't as holy as he seemed to be. They paid a woman to go up to his room to tempt him. Thomas simply drove the woman away, refusing to have anything to do with her.

After fifteen months, the family realized there was no way of changing his mind and he was allowed to go to Cologne, in present-day Germany, and to Paris to continue his studies. He was quite well built, and in class, he said so little that the other students nicknamed him "the Dumb Ox".

One day, Thomas's papers fell from his desk to the floor. Another student helped pick them up and noticed what Thomas had been writing.

"Look," he said, showing them around the class. "Our Thomas has understood everything we've been discussing after all."

The teacher realized how intelligent Thomas was. He said, "One day, that Dumb Ox will bellow so loudly he will shake the world."

Thomas did – partly because he himself became a famous university lecturer, but most of all because of the many books he wrote. Even those who disagree with some of his ideas respect his wisdom and his certainty that God is a loving father and that people can make themselves better by following his wishes.

He spent much of his life in Paris, where his advice was sought by many, including the French king Louis IX.

In 1272, Thomas went back to Naples. On Saint Nicholas's Day, he led a service in church. During the service, he saw a vision that moved him very deeply. "The end of my work has come," he announced. He wrote no more and died in March 1274.

Catherine of Siena

Catherine was born in 1347 and became a nun at the age of sixteen. She gained her reputation for holiness because of her good work among the poor of Siena and because of her visions and the strict life she led. She never learned to write, but more than four hundred of the letters she dictated have survived.

CATHERINE WAS ONLY six when she had her first vision. She knew he was Jesus, even though he was dressed not like a carpenter's son but in the fine robes usually worn by a pope. And she was equally certain that the two men with him were Saints John and Paul.

Catherine lived with her parents and her twenty-four brothers and sisters in the town of Siena, in northern Italy. Her father was a wealthy man who owned a business that dyed wool.

Like Clare of Assisi, Catherine was determined to become a nun, even though her parents wanted her to marry. She got her own way by cutting off her own hair to prove she was serious. As a punishment, her mother fired the family's servant and made Catherine dress as a maid and do all the household jobs. Catherine obeyed without ever complaining until her father decided she should be allowed to become a nun.

Instead of living with other nuns, Catherine

spent all her time in one room in her parents' home, eating hardly anything and often seeing more visions. Sometimes these were of Jesus. Other times, they were more like nightmares in which she felt the devil was coming to get her.

After three years, she had a special vision. This time, she seemed to see not only Jesus but also Mary, his mother. From this vision, she learned her life was not to be spent alone in prayer but in helping other people.

In those days, all Europe was being swept by the plague known as the Black Death. It was highly infectious, but Catherine had no hesitation in working among its victims. When a priest who was in charge of a hospital caught the illness and was thought to be close to death, she went bustling into his room.

"Get up, Father," she said. "Have something to eat. There's work to be done. It's no time for you to be lying in bed."

The priest was so surprised, he got up – and discovered he was no longer ill.

Catherine bustled around the city. She worked as a nurse. She dug graves for those who died of the plague and then buried them properly herself. She also continued to see visions, and then (in the year 1375) she began to dictate letters to anyone she thought needed her advice. She sent letters to kings, princes, and dukes all over Italy.

At this time, Italy was divided into a number of small but powerful and quarrelsome city-states. In particular, the city of Florence was a serious enemy of the city of Rome. There was another problem too. For the last seventy-five years, whoever was pope had been living at Avignon in France, rather than in Rome. Catherine thought that the pope should be in Rome, where they had always lived, and believed this would bring peace to Italy. So she wrote to Pope Gregory IX, explaining what he ought to do. Then she went to Avignon to tell him so in person. She failed to get him to make peace with Florence, but she did persuade him to return to Rome.

The next pope sent Catherine to Florence where she lived in considerable danger. But thanks to her determination and the respect everyone had for this holy woman, she finally established peace between Florence and Rome.

Thomas More

SAINT'S DAYS

22 JUNE
Roman Catholic Church

6 JULY
Anglican Churches

Thomas More was born in 1478. He trained as a
lawyer and entered parliament in 1504. King Henry
VIII soon became aware of his skills and appointed
him to several important jobs. Thomas had a strong
sense of right and wrong. He gave up his position
as lord chancellor when Henry divorced his wife,
Catherine of Aragon, and married Anne Boleyn.
Thomas also refused to accept Henry as head of the
church in England. He was executed in 1535.

B UT IT'S EASY. You just say what he wants you
to say." Margaret, a young woman in her
twenties, pleaded with her resolute father, Thomas
More.

"Margaret, my dear, it's not easy," he replied.

Not so very long before, Thomas More had been
lord chancellor – one of the most important men
in the land after King Henry VIII. He had been
powerful as well as popular. Now he had no job
and his life was in danger.

The trouble had started because King Henry
very much wanted to have a son to be king when
he died. He had a daughter named Mary but no
sons, and now the doctors said his wife, Queen
Catherine, could not have any more children. So
Henry claimed he had never been properly married
to her and divorced her.

Henry then married another woman, named Anne Boleyn. The pope, who (in those days) was the head of the whole church, said this was wrong. So too did Thomas More, who resigned as lord chancellor and refused to go to see Anne crowned queen. All this made Henry very angry, but Thomas was still popular with the ordinary people.

Two years later, the pope still said Anne Boleyn was not truly Henry's wife. So Henry persuaded parliament to make a law saying that in England he was head of the church, and that Anne was his legal wife and that her children (and not Mary's) should rule after him. Henry wanted all the important people in the country to swear by the Holy Bible that all this was true and right. But Thomas refused to swear this holy oath. This made the king angrier still.

What's more, he didn't want someone as popular as Thomas standing up against him – so he wanted Thomas "out of the way". Which was why Margaret was now trying to persuade her father to say the oath.

"It's easy," she said to her father. "It's just a few words. Say anything if it'll save you."

"But it's very wrong to say what's not true is true," her father insisted.

Some time later, he was locked up in a cold, dark

cell in the Tower of London. Friends came to see him. They too tried to get him to change his mind: "If you swear the oath, you can go free." Thomas kept silent.

A year after being put in prison, Thomas was charged with being a traitor to the king and the country – what's known as "treason." The punishment for treason was execution. He was taken to court and found guilty. Later, he was beheaded. His head was stuck on a post on London Bridge.

He could have saved himself. He didn't. It was a matter of conscience and Thomas More kept true to his conscience.

Good Lord, give me the grace to spend my life,
that when the day of my death shall come, though
I feel pain in my body, I may feel comfort in my soul;
and with faithful hope of thy mercy, with due love
toward thee, and charity toward the world, I may,
through grace, depart into thy glory.

A PRAYER BY THOMAS MORE

Ignatius of Loyola

SAINT'S DAY

31 JULY

Ignatius was born in the castle of Loyola in north-
eastern Spain in 1491. After being wounded in the
army, he decided on a life of holiness. In 1534, he
started the Society of Jesus, an order whose members
became known as the Jesuits. In the summer of 1556,
while in Rome, he suffered from fever. His doctors
did not think it was serious, but Ignatius knew he was
near death. He died on 31 July 1556.

IT ALL BEGAN with the cannonball. That was the
turning point for Ignatius. He was a soldier,
fighting for Spain against the French. That was
how he came to be wounded by the cannonball.
It hit him in the legs, tearing open his left calf and
breaking his right shin. He was captured by the
French, but they allowed him to be carried home
on a stretcher to Loyola, where his father was a
nobleman.

The doctors there found that one leg had been
badly set. It had to be rebroken and reset and then
stretched out by weights. It was very painful, and
Ignatius had to stay in bed for a long time. He
wanted something to read to pass the time. He
would have liked a romantic story of knights and
beautiful ladies. Instead, he was given a book of
stories about the saints.

Having read a few of the stories, including one

about Saint Francis, he suddenly said, "I could be as saintly as they were."

So when his leg had mended, instead of returning to the army, he gave away his uniform. He dressed himself as a beggar and went off to live in a mountain cave. Here he decided to get fit. Not physically fit but mentally fit. He trained his mind by praying seven hours a day. He wrote about what he was doing, describing it as his Spiritual Exercises.

He next decided he needed more education, so at the age of thirty-three, he went back to school in Barcelona and sat in a class of eleven-year-olds to learn Latin. He then journeyed to Rome and Jerusalem. He next set about serious study in Spanish universities and in Paris.

He was joined by six other students. They jointly made vows of poverty, chastity, and obedience. They also agreed to follow the Spiritual Exercises that Ignatius had written down and promised to carry out whatever jobs the pope might ask them to do. They felt they were to become an army or society, with Ignatius as its general, fighting for Jesus.

The pope (Paul III) liked the idea and so began the Society of Jesus. Since 1544, its members have been known as Jesuits. Within one hundred years, they had started five hundred schools and several universities.

Members of the Society also journeyed as missionaries to many distant countries. Some French Jesuits made the voyage to Canada with the aim of persuading Native peoples to become Christians. These included John de Brebeuf and Gabriel Lalemant, who were brutally murdered by a band of Iroquois in 1649.

Jesuits have sometimes been accused of being too strict, but ever since the days of Ignatius, they have thought of themselves as Christ's soldiers.

Teach us, good Lord, to serve you as you deserve; to give and not to count the cost; to fight and not to heed the wounds; to toil and not to seek for rest; to labour and not to ask for any reward, save that of knowing that we do your will.

A PRAYER OF SAINT IGNATIUS

Francis Xavier

SAINT'S DAY

3 DECEMBER

Francis was the son of a Spanish nobleman. He was born in 1506 in the castle of Xavier in the Basque country in northern Spain. After forming the Society of Jesus with Ignatius of Loyola, he journeyed to Rome and then to Portugal. He was sent to India as a missionary and visited several other countries, including Japan. During ten years in the Far East, he is said to have personally baptized several hundred thousand people. He died in 1552.

I T WAS A LONG, difficult voyage, sailing from Portugal right around the southern tip of Africa to India. While at sea, Francis remembered one day seven years earlier. He was then a student in Paris, where he had met a fellow Spanish student, Ignatius of Loyola. Ignatius had asked him a question from the Bible: "What profit is it if you gain the whole world but lose your own soul?" That was when Francis had given up everything to become one of the first seven members of the Society of Jesus. And that was why he was now sailing east to India.

The ship had set sail in April 1541 and it landed at Goa on the west coast of India in May 1542. There were some Christians there already: Europeans who'd come to trade. Francis was horrified at how cruelly they treated the local people and how wickedly they lived their own lives.

He began his work among these Europeans, but also preached to the local people. He would walk around the streets, ringing a little bell to call children to him. Then he would sit under an umbrella to guard against the sun and tell them Bible stories in their own language.

Francis was very practical. He helped people in hospital and prison. He became popular with the poorest people, sharing in their troubles by eating only rice and water and by sleeping only four hours a day.

Some time after his arrival there, he journeyed along the coast to visit other Portuguese settlements. To his surprise, he found a group of Indian people who were following traditions of Christian worship that had been used by the earliest Christians. These people were known as the Christians of Saint Thomas. They believed their faith had been brought to them centuries earlier by the same Thomas who had touched Jesus after he rose from the dead.

During the next few years, Francis made a trip to the Malay Peninsula and spent four months in a city called Malacca. While he was there, he met a Japanese man and heard stories about Japan, which no European had previously ever dared to visit.

Francis returned to India, determined to take the Christian message to Japan. He did this in 1549 with just five Christian helpers.

On his arrival, he spent a year learning the language. He then started to travel around the country. In some towns, the local ruler made him welcome. In several, he was given permission to preach. In one, he was allowed to turn a disused Buddhist temple into a church. But in other places, he was quickly turned away.

Nevertheless, Francis made at least two thousand converts to Christianity before he returned to India three years later. His work in Japan was continued by other missionaries until 1597, when the Japanese authorities turned against them, fearing they were the beginning of a European invasion.

Meanwhile, Francis decided he would next go to China. He set off with five other Jesuits and an interpreter. As foreigners were not then allowed into China, they landed secretly on an island called Sancian. Here Francis developed a fever. He died in early December 1552, aged just forty-six.

Elizabeth Ann Seton

SAINT'S DAY

4 JANUARY

Elizabeth was born in 1774. After only nine years
of marriage, she was widowed in 1803. She became
a Roman Catholic and in Emmitsburg formed a
community that became known as the Sisters of
Charity of St Joseph. Besides teaching, the nuns cared
for the poor and for orphaned children. Elizabeth died
in 1821, aged forty-seven. She was the first native-
born citizen of the United States of America to be
made a saint.

E LIZABETH WAS VERY beautiful with her dark
brown eyes and long dark hair. She was well
educated and popular. It was not surprising that
young William Seton fell in love with her. When
she fell adoringly in love with him too, they were
married and seemed certain to live happily ever
after.

Their life together began in a grand house on
Wall Street, in New York. William worked hard
at his family's shipping business. Elizabeth was
occupied with babies – five in all. But worries came
too.

William was no longer as healthy as he had
been. To make matters worse, his father died, and
the shipping business began doing badly. Two years
later, William and Elizabeth were bankrupt.

In 1803, their doctor said William might get

better if he got plenty of sea air by going on a long voyage. Elizabeth sold her remaining possessions (some silver, vases, and a few pictures) in order to pay the fares for herself, William, and their eldest child, Anna Maria. The other four children were left with William's sister, Rebecca.

They sailed across the Atlantic Ocean to Italy to stay with some friends. Disaster was waiting for them when they arrived at the port of Livorno. Because there had been an outbreak in New York of an illness known as yellow fever, they were not allowed to leave the port in case they were infectious. Instead, they were put in a stone tower and kept apart from all other people.

For forty days, Elizabeth looked after her husband, who was now coughing up blood. She tried to amuse Anna Maria with stories and games and she also held little prayer services. Eventually, they were free to join their friends, but William died soon afterward in Pisa, aged thirty-seven.

While waiting to return to America, Elizabeth went to church with her Italian friends. They were Roman Catholics. Elizabeth liked the services, even though she herself had grown up in the Anglican (or Episcopalian) Church.

Back in New York, she realized she had to earn a living to support her children. She did this by becoming a teacher. At the same time, she became a Roman Catholic, despite the opposition of family and friends. Then she was asked to start a girls' school. Other young women joined her and they formed a religious community, the first in the United States.

Elizabeth had been a wealthy young lady. But she'd had to face many hardships, including poverty and the loss of her husband. With each new problem, she found that God gave her strength and courage to cope.

What was the first rule of our dear Savior's life?
You know it was to do his Father's will.
Well, then, the first purpose of our daily work is to
do the will of God; secondly, to do it in the manner
he wills; and thirdly, to do it because it is his will.
We know certainly that our God calls us to a holy life.
We know that he gives us every grace, every abundant
grace; and though we are so weak of ourselves,
this grace is able to carry us through every
obstacle and difficulty.

ELIZABETH ANN SETON

John Bosco

31 JANUARY

*John Bosco was born in 1815. He had a dream of
creating an order – a dream he eventually achieved.
It was called the Salesian Order, or Society (after
Saint Francis of Sales). By the time of John's death in
1888, there were 250 houses of the Salesian Society
in all parts of the world, helping and educating
thousands of children. Don Bosco believed in kindness,
not punishment. He said, "As far as possible, avoid
punishing. Try to gain love before inspiring fear."*

E ARLY ONE DECEMBER day in 1841, a young
priest was about to take a service in a church
in the Italian city of Turin. From the back of the
church, he heard the caretaker saying, "What
are you doing here if you don't want to come to
Mass?"

A timid voice replied, "It's cold outside."

"That doesn't mean you can come in. Get out,
and be quick about it!"

The priest, whose name was John Bosco, called,
"Joseph, what are you doing? Call him back."

With a few bad-tempered mutterings, Joseph
persuaded the nervous boy to come back.

"Stay for Mass," the priest said to the boy gently,
"and we can talk later."

The youth's name was Bartollomea (or
Bartholomew) Garelli. He was sixteen and an

orphan. He had never been to school and could not read or write. After his parents had died, he'd come to the city, looking for work. John Bosco knew there were thousands of boys like this one in Turin. The lucky ones had somewhere to sleep. The others slept in doorways.

"Bart, would you like to learn to read if I were to teach you?"

"I suppose so."

"When you come, bring your friends."

This had been John Bosco's dream for a long time. He wanted to help, feed, and teach the street boys of Turin. By February, twenty boys were coming to his classes. Two years later, there were four hundred. Meanwhile, it was hard to find suitable meeting places.

They tried going to a public park, but local people complained about the noise. Then people started saying, "Don Bosco must be mad." ("Don" was a title often given to priests.)

"Why don't you cut down the number of boys?" asked another priest named Don Borel. "Limit yourself to twenty or so of the best-behaved ones."

"Don Borel, you speak of twenty boys when I see thousands. I dream of a huge school with beautiful buildings, large courtyards, a magnificent church. I picture classrooms; training shops where the boys can learn a trade. I even see some of them becoming priests themselves."

Word then spread that Don Bosco was indeed going mad. He would be taken away for a few weeks' rest in an asylum. Two priests went in their horse-drawn carriage to his house.

"Join us for a ride, Don Bosco," one of them said.

"Willingly," Don Bosco replied. "But first," he continued, "I have a plan I should like to discuss with you."

"Let's talk about this while we're riding around the city," said one of the priests craftily.

"Of course," Don Bosco replied.

"Get into the carriage then," they said.

"You first, please. You're more important than I am," he replied. No sooner were they seated in the coach than he slammed the door shut and called to the driver. "To the asylum, at once! These two gentlemen are expected there!"

Later, John Bosco's mother came to Turin to help him run a boarding house to shelter some of the boys. Gradually, dormitories were found where the rest could live safely. The city authorities recognized the good work John Bosco was doing and helped him to continue his work.

Bernadette Soubirous

*Marie Bernarde Soubirous (known as Bernadette) was
born in Lourdes in south-west France in 1844, the
first of six children. The family lived in great poverty.
Bernadette suffered from asthma and cholera and was
considered "backward". At the age of fourteen, she is
said to have had a series of eighteen visions of Mary,
the mother of Jesus. Bernadette became a nun and died
in 1879. Since then, Lourdes has become a popular site
of pilgrimage.*

I T ALL BEGAN one damp February afternoon.
Bernadette, her younger sister Toinette, and a
friend named Jeanne were walking beside a shallow
river, looking for firewood. They were near a small
cave, or grotto.

Seeing some fallen branches on the other side
of the river, Toinette and Jeanne took their shoes
off and waded through the icy water. Bernadette
hesitated. She had a cold and she didn't want to
bring on one of her asthma attacks. The wind
started blowing through the bushes near her. A soft
light appeared – and then Bernadette saw the Lady.

The other two girls returned to find Bernadette
looking terribly pale. When Toinette threw pebbles
at her, Bernadette seemed to wake up. Later,
Bernadette told Toinette about what she'd seen, and
Toinette told their mother. Next day, Jeanne told

everyone at school. The teachers told Bernadette to keep quiet or everyone would laugh at her.

During the following weeks, Bernadette claimed that she saw the Lady seventeen more times. Sometimes she took other children or grown-ups to the grotto. They heard Bernadette talking as if someone else were there, but they never saw the Lady.

After several appearances, the Lady spoke to Bernadette. It was a warning that she would never be happy in this world, but she would be happy in heaven. The people of the nearby town of Lourdes weren't sure what to make of it all. Some were disbelieving and said that Bernadette was a silly young girl or even mad. The local priest and doctor talked to her and examined her. So too did the police. But her story never altered.

One Saturday, the Lady appeared to Bernadette and told her to kiss the muddy ground near the river. Soon a spring of water appeared. On the same day, the Lady also told Bernadette that the priests must build a chapel or church at that place.

News of what was happening appeared in the newspapers. People began to come to Lourdes to see Bernadette and to visit the grotto. It became impossible for Bernadette to live a normal life.

After one of her final visions, Bernadette came

to understand that the Lady was Mary, the mother of Jesus. In due course, the church authorities agreed that Mary had actually appeared to young Bernadette.

Bernadette, meanwhile, wanted to escape from all the visitors, so she went to live in a convent. By now, she was very ill with severe asthma. In 1876, a great church was built near the grotto, but Bernadette did not attend the ceremony when the church was opened. "If only I could go to see and not be seen by the crowds," she said.

When she was very ill, one of the nuns in the convent asked her about having once been famous but now being hidden away. Bernadette replied that she felt very like a broom. "Our Lady used me and now I am put back in the corner."

Since that time, millions of pilgrims and tourists from all over the world have been to Lourdes to pray, or to bathe in the spring waters, or to seek healing from various illnesses. A committee of doctors investigates reports of healings that are claimed to be miracles.

Thérèse of Lisieux

Saint's Day

1 OCTOBER

Thérèse Martin was born in northern France in 1873, the daughter of a watchmaker. She entered the Carmelite convent of Lisieux in Normandy in 1888. Her book describing her way of serving God was published after her death in 1897, and has sold millions of copies around the world. It shows how anyone can serve God by doing everyday things in a spirit of love and kindness.

THÉRÈSE'S MOTHER DIED when Thérèse was young. She grew up with her father and her four older sisters. Marie, the oldest of the sisters, became a sort of mother to the family – except to little Thérèse. She thought of her next-oldest sister, Pauline, as her mother.

"You're my mother now," she said.

Pauline took special care of Thérèse, and perhaps because Thérèse was the youngest and often ill, they all spoilt her. When things didn't go as she wanted, Thérèse would burst into tears. Sometimes she would do this deliberately, just to get her own way.

When Thérèse was eight, Pauline decided to become a nun and live in a Carmelite convent in Lisieux, not far from where the family lived. Carmelite nuns believe that by staying in "Carmel" (as they call their convents), they can help people by praying for them. They hardly ever leave the convent and are allowed very few visitors. Thérèse was incredibly miserable about "losing" Pauline.

Thérèse slowly got used to life without her. Then, when she was thirteen, her oldest sister Marie said that she too was "going into Carmel". There were more tears.

But that Christmas, things changed. Thérèse decided that she herself would become a nun.

At first, there were problems. People said she was too young. But that autumn, her father took her on a visit to Rome. She was allowed to see the pope. When she was kneeling before him, she spoke up. "Holy Father," she said, "allow me to enter Carmel."

The pope seemed unsure what to say to this young girl. At last, he replied, "If it be God's will."

So, at the age of fifteen, Thérèse entered Carmel. I'm here for good! she thought. And she was happy.

But even though she was near her older sisters again, not everything was easy. Whenever Thérèse took her turn at doing the housework or weeding the garden, one of the older Carmelite nuns would criticize her.

Gradually, Thérèse learned not to answer back. One time, someone had left a little jar by a window and it had got broken. One of the other nuns supposed it had been Thérèse's fault. "You mustn't be so untidy. You must be much more careful!" the nun said.

Thérèse nearly said it wasn't her fault, but just stopped herself. "I'm sorry," was all she replied.

After five years, Thérèse's sister, Pauline, became prioress, or leader, of the nuns. One evening, she and Marie were talking with Thérèse about when they were children. Pauline told Thérèse to write down her memories. At first, Thérèse didn't want to, but she obediently agreed to do so. She had little spare time, so it took her more than a year. When she'd finished it, she gave it to Pauline.

Pauline showed it to Marie. Both sisters were impressed, but they felt that Thérèse should write more about her "little way" – her way of pleasing God by doing little things for other people and putting up with things without complaining.

But by now, Thérèse was seriously ill with tuberculosis. In those days, there was no cure. Even so, Marie encouraged Thérèse to finish writing her story. Although Thérèse was in great pain, she did so, completing it two months before she died.

Gabriel and Michael

SAINTS' DAYS

24 MARCH
Gabriel

29 SEPTEMBER
Michael
(the archangels Gabriel,
Raphael, and Michael are
now often celebrated together
on 29 September)

*Many people believe that angels are God's messengers.
Lucifer (also known as Satan, or the Devil) is said to
have once been an angel. But he rebelled against God
and so lost his place in heaven. He and his followers
are called "fallen angels". The other angels remained
loyal to God. The Bible says there are seven archangels
or chief angels. Gabriel and Michael (and also
Raphael) are the only ones regarded as saints.*

GABRIEL

OF ALL THE angels, Gabriel in particular has
been God's messenger. According to the
Bible, he spoke twice to a man named Daniel when
he was in prison and brought messages of hope. It
was Gabriel who told Zechariah that he was going
to be the father of John the Baptist.

Zechariah was working in the Temple in
Jerusalem, burning incense to make a sweet scent
while people were praying there. As he did this,
Gabriel appeared to him and told him what an
important person John would be. He also told him
that he must name him John. Because Zechariah
didn't really believe Gabriel, Zechariah lost the
ability to speak until his son was born. As soon as
Zechariah wrote down the words "His name is
John", he was able to speak again.

The most important message Gabriel ever

brought to earth was the message he brought to
Mary to tell her that she was to be the mother
of Jesus. Many people think it was also he who
appeared to the shepherds and told them to go and
worship Jesus in the manger at Bethlehem.

Gabriel is not just important to Jews and
Christians. Muslims (who call him Gibrail) believe
he dictated their holy book, the Qur'an, to the
prophet Muhammad.

MICHAEL

MICHAEL IS SAID to be one of the most
powerful of the angels. There is a story in
the Bible that long ago, the fallen angel Lucifer
tried to overthrow God. Lucifer is said to have
been a kind of dragon, but Michael, the first of the
archangels, was able to defeat him. This is how
the Bible describes the battle between Michael and
Lucifer:

"Then war broke out in heaven. Michael and
his angels fought against the dragon… The huge
dragon was thrown out – that ancient serpent,
called the Devil, or Satan, that deceived the whole
world. He was thrown down to earth, and all his
angels with him."

Michael appeared to humans in Old Testament
times. He spoke with Abraham and he appeared

to Moses. The Jews regarded him as their special protector, helping them to win battles against their enemies.

He is also important to Muslims and he is described in their holy book, the Qur'an, as having "wings of green emerald, covered with saffron hairs".

Christians think of him as the protector of the church. He is said to guard high places, which is perhaps why there are hills called St Michael's Mount in England, France, and Italy, and why many churches built on hills are named after him.

Although Saint Michael is known as "the protector of all people", he is believed to look after people especially at the time of their death. At one time, people thought he took care of the souls of people who had died by helping them to reach the new land of heaven. They imagined him taking them there by boat. This idea is remembered in the words of the song "Michael, Row the Boat Ashore".

Calendar of Saints' Days

SAINTS ARE USUALLY remembered on the anniversary of their death. The Eastern and Western Churches do not always remember saints on the same dates. However, unless a separate Eastern date is listed, days shown are universal. Days of remembrance may also vary from one country or district to another. They may also be moved in certain years so they do not coincide with Easter or another major festival.

JANUARY

1	Basil the Great *Eastern Church*
2	Basil the Great and Gregory Nazianzen
4	Elizabeth Ann Seton
7	Festival of John the Baptist *Eastern Church*
13	Kentigern (Mungo)
20	Sebastian
25	Gregory Nazianzen *Eastern Church*
25	Paul (conversion)
26	Timothy
26	Titus
28	Thomas Aquinas
30	Festival of Basil and Gregory Nazianzen (or Gregory the Theologian) *Eastern Church*
31	John Bosco

FEBRUARY

1	Brigid
2	Presentation of the Lord in the Temple (Mary's thanksgiving)

| 14 | Valentine |
| 24 | Ethelbert |

MARCH

1	David
17	Patrick
19	Joseph
20	Cuthbert
21	Benedict
24	Gabriel
25	Mary (the Annunciation)
26	Festival of the Angel Gabriel *Eastern Church*

APRIL

9	Mary, wife of Cleophas
16	Bernadette Soubirous
23	George
25	John Mark
29	Catherine of Siena
30	James the Apostle (brother of John) *Eastern Church*

MAY

1	Joseph the Worker
1	Philip and James the Less *Anglican Churches*
3	Philip and James the Less *Roman Catholic Church*
8	John the Evangelist *Eastern Church*
9	Christopher *Eastern Church*
9	Nicholas (translation of relics to Bari) *Eastern Church*
10	Simon the Apostle from Cana *Eastern Church*
21	Constantine the Great
21	Helena *Eastern Church*
25	Bede
25	The Three Marys (Mary of Magdala; Mary, the mother of James and John; and Mary, wife of Cleophas)
26	Augustine of Canterbury *Anglican Churches*
27	Augustine of Canterbury

JUNE

| 5 | Boniface |

9	Columba of Iona
10	Margaret of Scotland
11	Barnabas
11	Bartholomew (remembered with Barnabas) *Eastern Church*
13	Antony of Padua
22	Thomas More *Roman Catholic Church*
24	John the Baptist (his birthday)
29	Paul
29	(Simon) Peter
30	Festival of the Twelve Apostles (or disciples) *Eastern Church*

JULY

3	Thomas
6	Thomas More *Anglican Churches*
11	Benedict
22	Mary of Magdala
25	Christopher
25	James, son of Zebedee
26	Joachim and Anne
31	Ignatius of Loyola

AUGUST

5, 8, or 9	Oswald
10	Lawrence
11	Clare
15	Mary (the Assumption)
18	Helena
20	Bernard of Clairvaux
24	Bartholomew (Nathaniel)
28	Augustine of Hippo
29	John the Baptist (beheading)
31	Aidan

SEPTEMBER

3	Gregory
4	Cuthbert
8	Mary (her birthday)

21	Matthew
26	John the Evangelist (repose of) *Eastern Church*
29	Michael and All Angels

OCTOBER

1	Thérèse of Lisieux
4	Francis of Assisi
6	Thomas *Eastern Church*
9	James the Less *Eastern Church*
17	Ignatius of Antioch
18	Luke
22	Mary, the mother of James and John
28	Simon from Cana
28	Thaddeus (Jude)

NOVEMBER

5	Zechariah and Elizabeth
8	Festival of the angels Gabriel, Michael, and Raphael *Eastern Church*
11	Martin of Tours
14	Philip *Eastern Church*
16	Margaret of Scotland
16	Matthew *Eastern Church*
17	Hilda of Whitby
23	Clement
25	Catherine of Alexandria
30	Andrew

DECEMBER

3	Francis Xavier
6	Nicholas
8	Mary (the Immaculate Conception)
26	Stephen
27	John (apostle and evangelist)
27	Stephen *Eastern Church*
29	Thomas Becket